13 Colonies! 13 Years!

About the Authors

Mary Wheeler has more than 35 years of teaching experience in the Indiana public schools. She received her B.S. in Education from Ball State University and her M.S. in Education from Indiana University. Mary has been awarded the *Lilly Endowment* grant for Teacher Creativity. She has addressed the delegation of Indiana Historical Society members, detailing the use of music and drama to teach Indiana history. She is a longstanding member of the National Education Association, Indiana State Teachers' Association, Parent Teacher Organization, and the Shelby Eastern Classroom Teachers' Association.

Mary has been writing and producing educational activities, music, and musicals since 1979. She lives in Noblesville, Indiana, with her husband, John. She likes to spend her free time writing music and playing with her grandchildren.

Jill Terlep graduated from Purdue University with a B.S. in Economics. She has been a successful territory manager for both Hormel Foods and Bristol-Myers Squibb. Jill was responsible for teaching advanced wound care to nurses and physicians, along with patient teaching and counseling, while working with Bristol-Myers Squibb's medical products division. Jill conducted regular continuing education classes and nursing in-services. "Teaching, no matter what the subject, challenges your creativity and provides the opportunity to positively impact people's lives," says Jill.

Currently, Jill lives in Naperville, Illinois, with her husband, Jeff, and children, Drew and Lauren.

DATE DUE

PRINTED IN U.S.A.

13 Colonies!
13 Years!

Integrating Content Standards and the Arts to Teach the American Revolution

Mary Wheeler and Jill Terlep

Music by Mary Wheeler
Illustrations by Jill Terlep

Teacher Ideas Press, an imprint of Libraries Unlimited
Westport, Connecticut • London

Library of Congress Cataloging-in-Publication Data

Wheeler, Mary, 1944-
  13 colonies! 13 years! : integrating content standards and the arts to teach the American Revolution /
by Mary Wheeler and Jill Terlep.
    p. cm.
  Includes bibliographical references.
  ISBN 1-59158-414-0 (pbk. : alk. paper)
  1. History—Study and teaching (Elementary)—Activity programs. 2. United States—History—Study and
teaching (Elementary)—Activity programs 3. Education—Standards—United States. I. Terlep, Jill. II. Title.
III. Title: Thirteen colonies! Thirteen years!
curr LB1581.W44 2006
  372.89—dc22   2006023741

British Library Cataloguing in Publication Data is available.

Library of Congress Catalog Card Number: 2006023741
ISBN: 1-59158-414-0

First published in 2006

Libraries Unlimited/Teacher Ideas Press, 88 Post Road West, Westport, CT 06881
A Member of the Greenwood Publishing Group, Inc.
www.lu.com

Printed in the United States of America

The paper used in this book complies with the
Permanent Paper Standard issued by the National
Information Standards Organization (Z39.48–1984).

10   9   8   7   6   5   4   3   2   1

Contents

Acknowledgments

Thank You

... *Janet Compton, Carolyn Weintraut, and Linda Weintraut for help and much more.*

... *Michelle Barnes for knowing where to find the answer to every question, every time.*

... *Jann Beck for hard work and the fun times.*

... *Susan Hinkle for musical directions.*

... *Judy Cardisilaris for artistic props and sets.*

... *supervising and assisting staff members of Waldron Elementary School (WES).*

... *all of the students, parents, and families at WES who participated in the productions.*

... *all of the people who have helped and inspired us through the years.*

Special Acknowledgment and Thank You to

Gary Walters, Butler University, Indianapolis, Indiana,
for the musical arrangements and transcriptions.

and

John Wheeler and Jeff Terlep for your support, ideas, and faith in us.

This book is for Drew and Lauren.

Mary & Jill

Introduction

From the beginning of children's education, we use simple melodies to help them memorize their ABCs and learn to count. Songs and rhymes help children of all ages remember information. This resource book for your instruction about the American Revolution uses music, literature, and drama, along with other innovative and traditional methods of teaching. Thus, in *13 Colonies! 13 Years!* your students' learning takes place in an entertaining, enlightening, and exciting fashion.

With its very flexible format, this material can be presented in musical form or as rhyming verse. It can be used by an entire class in a regular setting or in individual learning stations for grades 4 through 8. It can be used as extra credit work or as a gifted and talented project. Depending on ability, students as young as second grade can participate in the production and the instructional activities. It is all up to you. See the *Where Do I Start?* section for more ideas.

The play at the end is another wonderful experience for your students. It can be acted in class, read silently, or performed for an audience.

Can you remember asking a parent or friend to "Watch me!" as you danced or sang or recited information as you were growing up? Even adults still love to entertain audiences. If you choose to stage the play, it is a memory that your students will treasure. Producing a program of this magnitude is a big project, but it is also a fun and satisfying one. It is impossible to forget the faces of the students, friends, and family members during the show.

From 1776 to 1789, those thirteen years included the events that provided the foundation for our great nation. Never have we been more proud of our past or more hopeful for our future. With this book you offer an opportunity for children … and adults … to celebrate our American heritage in a unique and unforgettable way.

13 Colonies! 13 Years!
They started with a declaration,
Ended with inauguration.
Let us have a celebration, NOW!

We'd love to hear from you. Enjoy!

Mary & Jill
maryandjill@teacherstoo.com
or
www.teacherstoo.com

Where Do I Start?

Our favorite element of *13 Colonies! 13 Years!* is its flexibility. What you do is up to you.

From the Declaration of Independence to the inauguration of George Washington, the thirteen years from 1776 to 1789 were filled with important and exciting events.

13 Colonies! 13 Years! is a teacher resource book containing eight original songs/rhymes about topics that shaped the American Revolution, such as *Constitutional Convention, Powder Your Wigs,* and *Frankly, Mr. Franklin.* Each song is accompanied by detailed background information and assessments.

Not only do students gain factual knowledge, they also become active learners as they research and discover a variety of subjects from the American Revolution period. At the end of the book, everything comes together in the educational play. All student materials are reproducible and designed to help you, the busy teacher.

Instruction can take place in a classroom, or students can work individually in learning stations or on their own time. The songs can be used as a complete set, independently, or in varied combinations— whatever suits your needs.

With the *Setting the Stage* pages, students in grades 4-8 can read the information either orally or silently and complete the paired worksheets independently or as a group. Sometimes, reading them aloud reinforces understanding and generates good discussions.

If you are using the book as a supplement to a text, you may choose to use only one or two of the *Setting the Stage* sheets and accompanying papers. Your curriculum needs determine which selections you pick.

Learning stations can start with one poem and its worksheet, or you can have several grouped together. Follow the work with a "research on your own" activity, too, using the reference or computer section of the library. Make answer cards for students to check their own work, or assign a teacher's helper.

Put *Setting the Stage* selections on students' desks the first thing in the morning. Pupils in grades 4-8 can "wake up" their brains while you prepare for the day.

Also, if you are not producing the play, give the music instructor two, three, or more of the songs to try in class. The music teacher might even want copies of *Setting the Stage* to create discussion on how the melodies and tempos of the songs match the background information. This is fun and educational for all ages. Written work can be followed up in either area.

In the *Research and Discovery* activities, teacher guidance will be needed for students in grades 4 and 5 to understand some of the concepts. For instance, talk about facts and opinions and have the class think of some concrete examples before assigning *George Washington Was the Best President.* Or discuss the table information and then allow children to complete *Changing Table, Parts I & II.* What kinds of buildings did cities have in the mid–eighteenth century? Build interest and let students identify starter ideas for *A City of Your Very Own.* Pupils in grade 6 and above should be able to complete the activities on their own. For additional information, older students can research on the Internet, in reference books, or with related materials.

Producing the play for large audiences will require help from adult volunteers for all age levels. Students in grades 7 and 8, however, can take charge of staging the play for a class. It is a great experience!

The book is divided into two sections: TEACHER RESOURCES and the PLAY.

TEACHER RESOURCES includes

- eight original songs/rhymes that can be sung or read.

- detailed background information, *Setting the Stage*, and accompanying worksheets for each song.

- colonial vocabulary lists of occupations, historical personalities, events, and documents with supplementary student worksheets.

- high-interest research and discovery activities that accommodate a variety of learning styles.

- many ideas for curriculum expansions.

- gifted and talented program suggestions.

The PLAY includes

- a musical program containing all eight original songs/rhymes.

- exciting characters that make the American Revolution fun to learn.

- a script that can be read silently, acted aloud in class, or performed for an audience.

- staging suggestions with everything needed to put on a full production, from cast lists and prop diagrams to costume ideas and performance tips.

- a Teacher Management section that has helpful time-savers like letters to send to parents, prop checklists, notation papers, and even more fun student activities.

We said in the beginning that flexibility is our favorite element of *13 Colonies! 13 Years!* Use any or every part of the text that you want. And back to the original question, "Where do I start?" … wherever **you** choose!

Text Correlations with National Standards for History

Standards in History for Grades K–4*

TOPIC 3

The History of the United States: Democratic Principles and Values and the People from Many Cultures Who Contributed to Its Cultural, Economic, and Political Heritage*

> Standard 4: How democratic values came to be, and how they have been exemplified by people, events, and symbols.

> Standard 5: The causes and nature of various movements of large groups of people into and within the United States, now and long ago.

> Standard 6: Regional folklore and cultural contributions that helped to form our national heritage.

PAGES	RESOURCE TITLES	STANDARDS
12	Revolutionary Era Overview	4-A, 4-B, 4-C, 4-D, 4-E, 5
15	13 Colonies! 13 Years!	4-A, 4-E
17	Frankly, Mr. Franklin	4-C, 4-D
22	Ballad of John Paul Jones	4-C, 4-E
25	Independence Battle Rap	4-B, 4-C, 4-E, 6-A
29	Wisdom Is Higher	4-C, 4-E, 5, 6-A
31	Powder Your Wigs	4-B
34	Constitutional Convention	4-A, 4-C, 4-D, 4-E
37	Sing in a Circle	4-E, 6-A
39	Colonial Terms—Vocabulary	4-A, 4-B, 4-E
45	Revolutionary Figures—Vocabulary	4-A, 4-B, 4-C, 4-E, 5
50	Occupations of the Era—Vocabulary	4-B, 5, 6-A
56	Events and Documents –Vocabulary	4-A, 4-B, 4-C, 4-D, 4-E
64	Settle Down and Get to Work	4-B, 5
65	Should Have Dunmore	4-A, 5
66	A City of Your Very Own	4-B, 5
67, 69	Whence You Came, Parts I and II	4-A, 4-C, 4-D, 4-E
70	Grand Convention (Plus One)	4-A, 5, 6-A
71	Help from Abroad	5
72	Yankee Doodle	5
73	Just the Facts	4-A, 4-C, 4-E, 5
75, 76	Ben Franklin Sails over the Ocean, Parts I and II	4-C, 5
78, 80	Changing Table, Parts I and II	5
81	Rally around Your Flag	4-E
82	We the (Other) People	4-A, 4-C
83	Electrical Problems	4-C
84	Runaway Hornbook	4-B, 6-A
85	It's a Match, Map	5
86	Cross Curriculum … More	Selections Vary
99	13 Colonies! 13 Years! Play	Entire

*Standards reprinted with permission from the National Center for History in the Schools, UCLA (http://nchs.ucla.edu).

Other valuable standards include *Building a United States History Curriculum* from the National Council for History Education at www.nche.net and *Expectations of Excellence: Curriculum Standards for Social Studies* from the National Council for the Social Studies at www.ncss.org.

From *13 Colonies! 13 Years! Integrating Content Standards and the Arts to Teach the American Revolution.* By Mary Wheeler and Jill Terlep. Music by Mary Wheeler. Illustrations by Jill Terlep. Westport, CT: Libraries Unlimited/Teacher Ideas Press. Copyright © 2006.

Text Correlations with National Standards for History

United States History Standards for Grades 5–12*

ERA 2: Colonization and Settlement (1585–1763)

Standard 1: Why the Americas attracted Europeans, why they brought enslaved Africans to their colonies, and how Europeans struggled for control of North America and the Caribbean

Standard 2: How political, religious, and social institutions emerged in the English colonies

Standard 3: How the values and institutions of European economic life took root in the colonies, and how slavery reshaped European and African life in the Americas

ERA 3: Revolution and the New Nation (1754–1820s)

Standard 1: The causes of the American Revolution, the ideas and interests involved in forging the revolutionary movement, and the reasons for the American victory.

Standard 2: The impact of the American Revolution on politics, economy, and society.

Standard 3: The institutions and practices of government created during the Revolution and how they were revised between 1787 and 1815 to create the foundation of the American political system based on the U.S. Constitution and the Bill of Rights.

PAGES	RESOURCE TITLES	ERAS/STANDARDS
12	Revolutionary Era Overview	Era 3: 1-A, 1-B, 1-C, 2-A, 3-A
15	13 Colonies! 13 Years!	Era 3: 1-A
17	Frankly, Mr. Franklin	Era 2: 2-C; Era 3: 1-C
22	Ballad of John Paul Jones	Era 2: 1-A; Era 3: 1-C
25	Independence Battle Rap	Era 3: 1-A, 1-C
29	Wisdom Is Higher	Era 2: 1-A, 3-C; Era 3: 2-C
31	Powder Your Wigs	Era 2: 1-A, 3-A; Era 3: 2-C
34	Constitutional Convention	Era 2: 2-A; Era 3: 2-A, 3-A
37	Sing in a Circle	Era 3: 1-A
39	Colonial Terms—Vocabulary	Era 2: 2-A; Era 3: 1-A, 1-B, 1-C, 3-A
45	Revolutionary Figures—Vocabulary	Era 2: 2-C; Era 3: 1-A, 1-C
50	Occupations of the Era—Vocabulary	Era 2: 1-A, 3-A; Era 3: 2-C
56	Events and Documents—Vocabulary	Era 2: 2-A; Era 3: 1-A, 1-B, 1-C, 2-A, - 2-B, 2-C, 3-A
64	Settle Down and Get to Work	Era 2: 3-A, 3-B, 3-C; Era 3: 2-C
65	Should Have Dunmore	Era 3: 1-B, 1-C, 2-C
66	A City of Your Very Own	Era 2: 2-A, 2-B, 3-A, 3-B
67, 69	Whence You Came, Parts I and II	Era 3: 1-A, 1-B, 3-A
70	Grand Convention (Plus One)	Era 3: 1-B, 1-C, 2-C, 3-A
71	Help from Abroad	Era 3: 1-C
72	Yankee Doodle	Era 3: 1-C
73	Just the Facts	Era 2: 2-A, 2-C, 3-B; Era 3: 1-A
75, 76	Ben Franklin Sails over the Ocean, Parts I and II	Era 2: 1-A, 2-C
78, 80	Changing Table, Parts I and II	Era 2: 2-A
81	Rally around Your Flag	Era 2: 2-A; Era 3: 1-C
82	We the (Other) People	Era 3: 1-C, 2-C
83	Electrical Problems	Era 2: 2-C
84	Runaway Hornbook	Era 2: 2-A
85	It's a Match	Era 3: 1-C
86	Cross Curriculum … More	Eras 2 and 3: Selections Vary
99	13 Colonies! 13 Years! Play	Eras 2 and 3

*Standards are reprinted with permission from the National Center for History in the Schools, UCLA (http://nchs.ucla.edu).

Other valuable standards include *Building a United States History Curriculum* from the National Council for History Education at www.nche.net and *Expectations of Excellence: Curriculum Standards for Social Studies* from the National Council for the Social Studies at www.ncss.org.

From 13 Colonies! 13 Years! Integrating Content Standards and the Arts to Teach the American Revolution. By Mary Wheeler and Jill Terlep. Music by Mary Wheeler. Illustrations by Jill Terlep. Westport, CT: Libraries Unlimited/Teacher Ideas Press. Copyright © 2006.

Text Correlations with Standards for the English Language Arts

National Council of Teachers of English/International Reading Association*

"A strong grasp of content in the English language arts is vital, but knowledge alone is of little value if one has no need to, or cannot, apply it. The ability to use language for a variety of purposes is therefore another essential part of the learning experience. We believe that a central goal of English language arts education is to ensure that students are able to use language to address their own needs as well as the needs of their families, their communities, and the greater society. In particular, we recommend a focus in English language arts education on four purposes of language use: for obtaining and communicating information, for literary response and expression, for learning and reflection, and for problem solving and application."

PAGES	RESOURCE TITLES	STANDARDS
12	Revolutionary Era Overview	1, 2, 3
15	13 Colonies! 13 Years!	1, 2, 3, 4
17	Frankly, Mr. Franklin	1, 2, 3, 4, 5, 6, 9
22	Ballad of John Paul Jones	1, 2, 3
25	Independence Battle Rap	1, 2, 3, 4
29	Wisdom Is Higher (A Tribute to Phillis Wheatley)	1, 2, 3, 4, 5, 9, 12
31	Powder Your Wigs	1, 2, 3, 4, 5
34	Constitutional Convention	1, 2, 3, 4, 5
37	Sing in a Circle	1, 2, 3, 6
39	Colonial Terms—Vocabulary	1, 2, 3, 4, 5, 6, 8
45	Revolutionary Figures—Vocabulary	1, 2, 3, 4, 5,
50	Occupations of the Era—Vocabulary	1, 2, 3, 4, 5, 6, 7, 9
56	Events and Documents—Vocabulary	1, 2, 3, 4, 5, 6, 7
64	Settle Down and Get to Work	1, 2, 3, 4, 6
65	Should Have Dunmore	1, 2, 3, 4, 9, 11
66	A City of Your Very Own	1, 2, 3, 4, 6
67, 69	Whence You Came, Parts I and II	1, 2, 3, 9, 11, 12
70	Grand Convention (Plus One)	1, 4, 5, 7, 9
71	Help from Abroad	1, 2, 3, 5, 7, 8, 9
72	Yankee Doodle	1, 6
73	Just the Facts	1, 2, 3, 5
75. 76	Ben Franklin Sails over the Ocean, Parts I and II	1, 5, 11, 12
78, 80	Changing Table, Parts I and II	1, 3, 4, 7
81	Rally around Your Flag	1.5
82	We the (Other) People	1, 2, 3, 5, 6, 7, 8, 9, 11, 12
83	Electrical Problems	4
84	Runaway Hornbook	4, 5, 6
85	It's a Match, Map	1, 4
86	Cross Curriculum ... More	Selections Vary
99	13 Colonies! 13 Years! The Play	1, 2, 3, 11, 12

Text Correlations with National Standards for Arts Education

National Standards for Arts Education—Dance, Music, Theatre, Visual Arts*

"All peoples, everywhere, have an abiding need for meaning—to connect time and space, experience and event, body and spirit, intellect and emotion. People create art to make these connections, to express the otherwise inexpressible. A society and a people without the arts are unimaginable."

FOR GRADES K–4 AND GRADES 5–8

PAGES	RESOURCE TITLES	CONTENT STANDARDS
15	13 Colonies! 13 Years!	Visual Arts 1, 2, 3, 4, 5
37	Sing in a Circle	Visual Arts 1, 2, 3, 4, 5
66	A City of Your Very Own	Visual Arts 1, 2, 3, 4, 6
72	Yankee Doodle	Music 1, 4, 9
73	Just the Facts	Visual Arts 1, 3, 5
81	Rally around Your Flag	Visual Arts 1, 2, 3, 4, 6
82	We the (Other) People	Visual Arts 1, 2, 3, 4, 5, 6; Music (Varies 1, 2) 8, 9
85	It's a Match, Map	Visual Arts 1, 2, 3, 4, 6
86	Cross Curriculum … More (Varied Selections)	Dance 1, 2, 3, 5, 7; Music 1, 2, 3, 5, 6, 8, 9; Theatre 1, 2, 3, 4, 5; Visual Arts 1, 2, 3, 4, 5, 6
99	*13 Colonies! 13 Years!* the Play, Grades K–4	Dance 1, 2, 3, 4; Music 1, 2, 5, 6, 7, 8, 9; Theatre 2, 3, 4, 7, 8; Visual Arts 1, 2, 3, 4, 5, 6
99	*13 Colonies! 13 Years!* The Play, Grades 5–8	Dance 1, 2, 3, 4, 5; Music 1, 2, 5, 6, 7, 8, 9; Theatre 2, 3, 4, 7, 8; Visual Arts 1, 4, 5, 6

* From *National Standards for Arts Education*. Copyright © 1994 by Music Educators National Conference (MENC). Used by permission. The complete National Arts Standards and additional materials relating to the Standards are available from MENC—The National Association for Music Education, 1806 Robert Fulton Drive, Reston, VA 20191.

Teacher Resources

Background Information and Rhymes,
Guided Activities

Song and Rhyme Synopsis

Memorize the names of the 13 colonies and do it in festive style in *13 Colonies! 13 Years!*

Can Benjamin Franklin offer advice for solving today's problems? Of course. In *Frankly, Mr. Franklin,* the diplomat spouts quotations from his own *Poor Richard's Almanack.*

"I have not yet begun to fight!" In *The Ballad of John Paul Jones,* the naval officer shouts those stirring words, and we celebrate his bravery.

From Lexington to Concord to victory at Yorktown, be a Yankee Doodle and march to the cadence of *Independence Battle Rap.*

Wisdom Is Higher—so climb the steps with Phillis Wheatley, African American poet.

Get ready for lots of action with *Powder Your Wigs.* Everyone does aerobic movements that match the motions of colonial craftsmen.

Thank George Washington, James Madison, Gouverneur Morris, and all the delegates to the *Constitutional Convention.*

In *Sing in a Circle* rally around the soaring American eagle.

Revolutionary Era Overview

After the French and Indian War, the colonists wanted to move west into newly acquired land between the Appalachian Mountains and the Mississippi River. However, the British worried that new settlements would anger the Indians. Britain, under King George III, issued the Proclamation of 1763, forbidding colonists to settle the former French lands. The Proclamation angered the colonists.

Taxation without Representation

To help pay off its wartime debt, Parliament also decided to tax the colonies. Especially inflaming the Americans was the Stamp Act of 1765. In it, tariffs were placed on all kinds of printed matter, such as newspapers, documents, ministers' sermons, even playing cards. The Sons of Liberty was organized by colonial men to protest this tax that many believed was unfair. Protests grew more violent, and soon Parliament repealed the tax.

The Townshend Duties of 1767 were collected on items such as lead, paint, paper, and tea. After their enactment a colonial boycott was organized. When Britain sent soldiers to control the American protest, the Boston Massacre took place on March 5, 1770. Crispus Attucks, an African American, was among the few colonists killed.

It's Tea Time

With the Tea Act of 1773, Britain found a way to get colonists to buy tea again *and* pay a tax. But the Committees of Correspondence, formed to watch and report British activities to members in the colonies, sent the news. The Sons of Liberty prevented ships from docking in Philadelphia and New York City. On December 16, 1773, the Boston Tea Party was held. Patriots, dressed as Indians, threw tea from British ships into Boston Harbor.

News of the Boston Tea Party enraged King George III and Parliament. In 1774 Parliament passed several laws to punish the Americans. These Intolerable Acts ended town meetings, removed some power from the Massachusetts Assembly, and closed Boston Harbor until Patriots paid for the tea. Britain also sent more troops for enforcement, and under the Quartering Act, ordered colonists to house and feed them.

The Colonies Convene

The First Continental Congress was held in 1774 in Philadelphia with delegates from 12 colonies represented—every one except Georgia. Among the delegates were George Washington, John Adams, John Hancock, Samuel Adams, Patrick Henry, and John Jay. Members drew up a list of complaints against King George III and Parliament. Colonists were coming together as Americans.

From *13 Colonies! 13 Years! Integrating Content Standards and the Arts to Teach the American Revolution.* By Mary Wheeler and Jill Terlep. Music by Mary Wheeler. Illustrations by Jill Terlep. Westport, CT: Libraries Unlimited/Teacher Ideas Press. Copyright © 2006.

The British Are Coming!

Patriots began preparing to fight for their rights. Farmers and townspeople, called Minutemen, began to drill with their muskets. On April 18, 1775, Paul Revere, William Dawes, and Dr. Samuel Prescott rode to Lexington, warning colonists along the way of a British march. The first battles of the Revolutionary War occurred in Lexington and Concord between the British (Redcoats) and the Minutemen. George Washington was chosen by the Second Continental Congress to lead the Continental Army.

We Hold These Truths …

Common Sense, a pamphlet by Thomas Paine, was published in January 1776. It was written in everyday language, and it attacked the actions of King George III and argued for colonial independence. *Common Sense* was read by probably half of the colonists, and many agreed with it. On July 4, 1776, Congress adopted the Declaration of Independence.

Battling the British

Bunker Hill, Boston, Fort Ticonderoga—the early battles of the Revolutionary War were fought in the northern colonies. When the fighting shifted to the middle colonies, George Washington's Continental Army was driven from New York. The Patriots retreated across New Jersey but were victorious in Trenton and Princeton in the winter of 1776–1777. After campaigns in New York, Vermont, and Pennsylvania, the Patriots spent a bitter winter at Valley Forge in 1777–1778. In 1779, the war shifted to the southern colonies. With the aid of French troops and warships, Washington led the Continental Army to victory at Yorktown. On October 19, 1781, the British Army surrendered.

There were six-and-a-half years of fighting during the American Revolution, from April 19, 1775, through October 19, 1781. About 8,000 Americans were killed or wounded, and total cost of the war to Americans was approximately $200 million dollars.

From *13 Colonies! 13 Years! Integrating Content Standards and the Arts to Teach the American Revolution.* By Mary Wheeler and Jill Terlep. Music by Mary Wheeler. Illustrations by Jill Terlep. Westport, CT: Libraries Unlimited/Teacher Ideas Press. Copyright © 2006.

Creating a Government

Delegates to the Second Continental Congress wrote the Articles of Confederation, a national plan of government. Placed into effect in 1781, the Articles left governmental powers to the states. However, the new central government was weak—no power to tax, raise an army, or regulate trade. Several farmers, led by Daniel Shay, protested against Massachusetts taxation in 1787. Shay's Rebellion helped convince many Americans that a stronger central government was needed.

We the People ...

The Constitutional Convention opened on May 25, 1787, at Independence Hall in Philadelphia. Delegates represented 12 of 13 states, and they chose George Washington as their chairman. The Constitution created a federal system of government. Three branches—legislative, executive, and judicial—provided the system with checks and balances. Penned more than 200 years ago, it is the oldest written constitution in the world today.

After the Constitution was ratified by the states, elections were held to choose a president and members of Congress. George Washington was chosen by the people as the first president of the United States, and he was inaugurated at Federal Hall in New York City on April 30, 1789.

13 Colonies! 13 Years! 13 Colonies! 13 Years!

They started with a declaration,

Ended with inauguration.

Let us have a celebration, NOW!

From *13 Colonies! 13 Years! Integrating Content Standards and the Arts to Teach the American Revolution.* By Mary Wheeler and Jill Terlep. Music by Mary Wheeler. Illustrations by Jill Terlep. Westport, CT: Libraries Unlimited/Teacher Ideas Press. Copyright © 2006.

The Revolutionary Overview Poem

In 1763, King George the Third started events in motion.
He made a proclamation that caused a colonial commotion.
He forbid the colonists to move west into newly acquired lands.
This was the first of many acts taking choice out of colonists' hands.

The Stamp Act of 1765 was a tax to pay off England's war debt.
The tax on all printed materials made the colonists upset.
The Sons of Liberty organized. They believed that the tax was wrong.
Parliament repealed this law, but passed several more before long.

The Townshend Duties of 1767 taxed lead, paint, paper, and tea.
The Boston Massacre in 1770 was a result of these unfair duties.
The Tea Act of 1773 brought a new tax for the colonists to bear.
The Boston Tea Party was held to show England the act wasn't fair.

Next came the Intolerable Acts, as punishment for the tea that was lost.
England closed Boston Harbor until they paid for the tea they had tossed.
The Massachusetts Assembly was weakened, and town meetings were through.
The Quartering Act meant housing the British troops; that they didn't want to do.

At the First Continental Congress, delegates took a stand.
It was time to join as Americans to escape King George the Third's iron hand.
Many Patriots prepared to fight for their rights with ardor and resolution.
Lexington, April 1775, it was the battle that began the Revolution.

Thomas Paine wrote Common Sense for many of the colonists to read.
The Second Continental Congress chose George Washington to lead.
The Declaration of Independence was signed in 1776 on the Fourth of July.
It was determination and colonial spirit on which they would now rely.

From 13 Colonies! 13 Years! Integrating Content Standards and the Arts to Teach the American Revolution. By Mary Wheeler and Jill Terlep. Music by Mary Wheeler. Illustrations by Jill Terlep. Westport, CT: Libraries Unlimited/Teacher Ideas Press. Copyright © 2006.

Revolutionary Era Overview

Circle the letter of the correct answer.

1. In the mid–18th century, the British worried that new settlements between the Appalachian Mountains and Mississippi River would anger the

            a. colonists.   b. Indians.   c. slaves.

2. During the Revolutionary Era, Britain's reigning king was

            a. King Andrew II.   b. King Charles IV.   c. King George III.

3. The Proclamation of 1763 forbid colonists to

    a. settle former French lands.
    b. own their own land.
    c. travel to Britain.

4. In the 1760s, British Parliament decided to tax colonists because Britain needed to

    a. construct new roads and government buildings.
    b. explore new territories to add to the British Empire.
    c. pay off its wartime debts.

5. The British Stamp Act of 1765 made colonists angry because it taxed items, such as

    a. guns, ships, and homes.
    b. income, jewelry, and train travel.
    c. newspapers, ministers' sermons, and playing cards.

6. To protest the tax of 1765 that many thought unfair, colonial men organized the

            a. Boston Redcoats.   b. Sons of Liberty.   c. British Minutemen.

7. On March 5, 1770, the Boston Massacre occurred after a colonial boycott of the

    a. Townshend Duties of 1767.
    b. Constitution.
    c. Articles of Confederation.

8. Among the few colonists killed during the Boston Massacre was an African American named

            a. William Dawes.   b. Benjamin Franklin.   c. Crispus Attucks.

9. The Boston Tea Party was held on December 16, 1773, and Patriots dressed up as

            a. women.   b. British soldiers.   c. Indians.

10. When King George III learned of the Boston Tea Party, he

            a. laughed.   b. cried.   c. got angry.

11. To punish the Americans for staging the Boston Tea Party, in 1774 Parliament passed the

            a. Stamp Act.   b. Intolerable Acts.   c. Townshend Acts.

12. The First Continental Congress was held in

        a. New York City.   b. Boston.   c. Philadelphia.

13. The farmers and townspeople who first prepared to fight for colonial rights were called the

        a. Minutemen.   b. Redcoats.   c. British.

14. Calling for colonial independence, Thomas Paine wrote a pamphlet called

    a. the Declaration of Independence.
    b. *Common Sense.*
    c. *Revolutionary Ideas.*

15. Congress adopted the Declaration of Independence on

        a. January 1, 1776.   b. April 18, 1775.   c. July 4, 1776.

16. The British Army surrendered after the Battle of

        a. Yorktown.   b. Bunker Hill.   c. New York.

17. The American Revolution lasted for

        a. 2 years.   b. 6 1/2 years.   c. 10 years.

18. A Second Continental Congress did not create a central government that was

    a. strong enough.
    b. big enough.
    c. wise enough.

19. In 1787, the Constitutional Convention created a federal system of government with

    a. one area.
    b. three branches.
    c. five sections.

20. Inaugurated at Federal Hall in New York City on April 30, 1789, was the first president of the United States,

    a. Abraham Lincoln.
    b. John F. Kennedy.
    c. George Washington.

From *13 Colonies! 13 Years! Integrating Content Standards and the Arts to Teach the American Revolution.* By Mary Wheeler and Jill Terlep. Music by Mary Wheeler. Illustrations by Jill Terlep. Westport, CT: Libraries Unlimited/Teacher Ideas Press. Copyright © 2006.

13 Colonies! 13 Years!

Setting the Stage

The years 1776–1789 were 13 of the most formidable in United States history. The Declaration of Independence, Revolutionary War, Constitutional Convention, and Presidential Inauguration—it was an exhilarating era when our nation was born.

Bells, including the Liberty Bell as it was called later, rang in celebration of special occasions. Inscribed on the Liberty Bell are the words, "Proclaim liberty throughout the land and unto all the inhabitants thereof."

King George III took the throne in 1760. During his reign, the colonies went from being loyal subjects to dissident rebels. Tensions increased as King George III and Parliament imposed tariffs and restrictions on the colonies. Eventually, armed conflict broke out, and the arts colonies began to fight for their independence.

The thirteen original colonies were Massachusetts, Pennsylvania, Connecticut, Delaware, North Carolina, South Carolina, Georgia, New Hampshire, New York, New Jersey, Maryland, Virginia, and Rhode Island.

13 Colonies! 13 Years!

1776 to 1789
13 colonies, 13 years! 13 colonies, 13 years!
They started with a declaration,
Ended with inauguration.
Let us have a celebration, NOW!
13 colonies, 13 years! 13 colonies, 13 years!

Massachusetts, Pennsylvania, Connecticut, and Delaware,
North Carolina, South Carolina, Georgia—they all were there.

New Hampshire, New York, and New Jersey—
Everywhere church bells were heard.
Maryland, Virginia, and tiny Rhode Island—
They all opposed King George the Third.

1776 to 1789
13 colonies, 13 years! 13 colonies, 13 years!
They started with a declaration,
Ended with inauguration.
Let us have a celebration, NOW!

13 Colonies! 13 Years!

Name the 13 original colonies in alphabetical order.

1. _____   8. _____

2. _____   9. _____

3. _____   10. _____

4. _____   11. _____

5. _____   12. _____

6. _____   13. _____

7. _____

Draw the Liberty Bell and write the inscription on it.

Frankly, Mr. Franklin

Setting the Stage

Benjamin Franklin (1706–1790) was one of 17 children born to a Boston soap and candle maker. Although Franklin had little formal schooling, he became one of the most famous international figures of the era.

As a successful Philadelphia printer, Franklin annually published the very popular *Poor Richard's Almanack*. Selling as many as 10,000 copies a year for 25 years, the almanacks were a collection of witty and wise short sayings, calendars, and miscellaneous information. His lucrative business career helped him achieve financial independence at a relatively early age.

Franklin improved methods of paving, cleaning, lighting, and heating in the city of Philadelphia. His civic contributions also included establishing the first public subscription library and fire company.

Benjamin Franklin was an inventor. Among his most well known inventions are lightning rods, bifocal glasses, and Franklin stoves.

He officially served the city of Philadelphia and also the colonial legislature of Pennsylvania. During the Stamp Act crisis, he became the spokesman for America's rights in London. Franklin was named a member of the Continental Congress in May 1775, and he served on a committee to draft the Declaration of Independence. After helping to negotiate the Treaty of Paris, he became a representative to the Constitutional Convention.

A distinguished figure in American history, Benjamin Franklin was a diplomat, publisher, philosopher, author, scientist, politician, and philanthropist. Today, more than two centuries after his death, he remains a symbol of American civilization.

Frankly, Mr. Franklin

Frankly, Mr. Franklin, we need some good advice.
Some almanack quotations from Poor Richard would be nice.
Help us put our minds at ease
With these people; tell us please.
Frankly, Mr. Franklin, we need some good advice.

Sam invited company, served cake and soda pop.
Because he never smiled at all his party was a flop.
Mr. Franklin:
"If you would have guests merry with cheer, be so yourself, or so at least appear."

From *13 Colonies! 13 Years! Integrating Content Standards and the Arts to Teach the American Revolution.* By Mary Wheeler and Jill Terlep. Music by Mary Wheeler. Illustrations by Jill Terlep. Westport, CT: Libraries Unlimited/Teacher Ideas Press. Copyright © 2006.

Susie did her math each day; she wanted a good grade.
But since she did not check her work, a "C" is what she made.
Mr. Franklin:
"Well done is twice done."

Frankly, Mr. Franklin, we need some good advice.
Some almanack quotations from Poor Richard would be nice.
Help us put our minds at ease
With these people; tell us please.
Frankly, Mr. Franklin, we need some good advice.

Mary was a lazy girl, would not get out of bed.
"We can't depend on her at all," her worried mother said.
Mr. Franklin:
"Lost time is never found again."

Alice was a follower. She seldom used her mind.
When others "jumped into a lake," she wasn't far behind.
Mr. Franklin:
"There are lazy minds as well as lazy bodies."

Frankly, Mr. Franklin, we need some good advice.
Some almanack quotations from Poor Richard would be nice.
Help us put our minds at ease
With these people; tell us please.
Frankly, Mr. Franklin, we need some good advice.

"I am smarter than you are," that bragger, Bart, would say.
He wasn't smart enough to know why people stayed away.
Mr. Franklin:
"People who are wrapped up in themselves make small packages."

Frankly, Mr. Franklin, we need some good advice.
Some almanack quotations from Poor Richard would be nice.
Help us put our minds at ease
With these people; tell us please.
Frankly, Mr. Franklin, we need some good advice.

From *13 Colonies! 13 Years! Integrating Content Standards and the Arts to Teach the American Revolution.* By Mary Wheeler and Jill Terlep. Music by Mary Wheeler. Illustrations by Jill Terlep. Westport, CT: Libraries Unlimited/Teacher Ideas Press. Copyright © 2006.

NAME _____ DATE_____

Frankly, Mr. Franklin

It's all about Benjamin Franklin … True or False?

1. _____ He had no brothers or sisters.

2. _____ His father was a doctor.

3. _____ He annually published *Poor Richard's Almanack*.

4. _____ He did not have very much money until late in life.

5. _____ Ben improved the lighting in Philadelphia.

6. _____ Among his inventions are bifocals and lightning rods.

7. _____ He was against the Stamp Act that England imposed.

8. _____ He did not attend the Constitutional Convention.

9. _____ He worked as a diplomat for the United States in Asia.

10. _____ He wrote *Common Sense.*

11. _____ *Poor Richard's Almanack* contained diagrams of prehistoric animals.

12. _____ He is a distinguished figure in American history.

13. _____ He earned a college degree.

14. _____ Calendars were included in *Poor Richard's Almanack.*

15. _____ He became a famous international figure.

16. _____ He helped to negotiate the Treaty of Washington.

17. _____ He officially served the colonial legislature of Virginia.

18. _____ Over 100,000 copies of *Poor Richard's Almanack* were sold each year.

19. _____ "Well done is twice done" is a familiar Franklin quote.

20. _____ In London, he spoke on behalf of American rights.

From *13 Colonies! 13 Years! Integrating Content Standards and the Arts to Teach the American Revolution.* By Mary Wheeler and Jill Terlep. Music by Mary Wheeler. Illustrations by Jill Terlep. Westport, CT: Libraries Unlimited/Teacher Ideas Press. Copyright © 2006.

Wisdom of the Ages

Match the situation with the saying from *Poor Richard's Almanack*.

Haste makes Waste.

No gains without pains.

You may delay, but Time will not.

Well done is better than well said.

The Things which hurt, instruct.

'Tis easier to prevent bad habits than to break them.

He that won't be counsell'd, can't be help'd.

He that cannot obey, cannot command.

Observe all men; thyself the most.

1.   John bragged that he was a great basketball player, but he did not score any points in the last five games.

     _____

2.   Mary noticed that a lot of children in her class did not do a good job on the assignment. Mary's grade was C–.

     _____

3.   Jim said, "I'm strong enough. I don't need to exercise or practice." He lost his first wrestling match.

     _____

4.   Susan did not practice her clarinet solo. When the concert was held on Thursday, she shrank down in her chair after she forgot her notes. On Saturday morning, Susan was in her room practicing songs at 8:00 A.M.

     _____

5.   Alice would not listen to her parents when they wanted to talk about her behavior. She got in trouble at school.

     _____

6.   Rex was too busy to pick the tomatoes when they first ripened. He had to throw several away a few days later.

     _____

7. Ralph finished his lessons every night and listened closely to his teacher. He became a well-respected policeman.

   _____

8. The builder finished constructing the house in record-breaking time. The homeowner needed to repair the plumbing, siding, and flooring often.

   _____

9. Don't smoke cigarettes or try drugs.

   _____

Choose one of the sayings and write your own example.

Do me the favour to deny me at once.

One To-day is worth two To-morrows.

Be slow in choosing a friend, slower in changing.

Keep thy shop, and thy shop will keep thee.

Saying: _____

_____

Example:

_____

_____

_____

_____

_____

_____

_____

_____

_____

From *13 Colonies! 13 Years! Integrating Content Standards and the Arts to Teach the American Revolution.* By Mary Wheeler and Jill Terlep. Music by Mary Wheeler. Illustrations by Jill Terlep. Westport, CT: Libraries Unlimited/Teacher Ideas Press. Copyright © 2006.

The Ballad of John Paul Jones

Setting the Stage

John Paul Jones was born in 1747 in Scotland. The son of a gardener, John Paul (his real name) left his country as a young lad to be a seaman. Later, John moved to the colonies and changed his name to John Paul Jones.

When the Revolution started, John joined the Continental Navy, and he was commissioned as a captain in June 1777. Because there was little money to fund the navy, Jones took command of a refitted, aging merchant ship that was donated by France. He renamed the ship *Bonhomme Richard* in honor of Benjamin Franklin and his *Poor Richard's Almanack*.

"I have not yet begun to fight." John Paul Jones reportedly shouted those words during the famous battle with a British warship. On September 23, 1779, Jones and his crew captured the *Serapis* and sailed her into port. *Bonhomme Richard* sank after the battle ended, and Captain Jones became the first American naval hero.

John Paul Jones died in 1792, and he is buried at the Naval Academy in Annapolis, Maryland.

The Ballad of John Paul Jones

John Paul Jones was a hero;
He battled shore to shore.
He named his ship Bonhomme Richard
And sailed it off to war.

John Paul Jones left Scotland 'cause he wanted to be free.
He settled in the colonies, but John Paul loved the sea.
Americans refused a tax and firmly took a stand.
In the Continental Navy, John accepted a command.

John Paul Jones was a hero;
He battled shore to shore.
He named his ship Bonhomme Richard
And sailed it off to war.

From *13 Colonies! 13 Years! Integrating Content Standards and the Arts to Teach the American Revolution.* By Mary Wheeler and Jill Terlep. Music by Mary Wheeler. Illustrations by Jill Terlep. Westport, CT: Libraries Unlimited/Teacher Ideas Press. Copyright © 2006.

John's crew began to fire upon the mighty British fleet.
Although his ship was damaged, John would not accept defeat.
Captain Jones stood up and called above the cannons' roar,
"I have not yet begun to fight," and so they fought some more.

John Paul Jones was a hero;
He battled shore to shore.
He named his ship Bonhomme Richard
And sailed it off to war.

Bonhomme Richard was sinking fast. John took his valiant crew
Aboard a beaten English ship that knew that it was through.
John lost his ship, but won the fight. When all the smoke had cleared,
The news of John Paul's victory reached home, and people cheered.

John Paul Jones was a hero;
He battled shore to shore.
He named his ship Bonhomme Richard
And sailed it off to war.

"I have not yet begun to fight. I have not yet begun to fight."
His words still echo in our ears.
"I have not yet begun to fight. I have not yet begun to fight."
We do remember after all these years.

"I have not yet begun to fight. I have not yet begun to fight."
His words still echo in our ears.
"I have not yet begun to fight. I have not yet begun to fight."
We do remember after all these years.

From *13 Colonies! 13 Years! Integrating Content Standards and the Arts to Teach the American Revolution.* By Mary Wheeler and Jill Terlep. Music by Mary Wheeler. Illustrations by Jill Terlep. Westport, CT: Libraries Unlimited/Teacher Ideas Press. Copyright © 2006.

The Ballad of John Paul Jones

What? When? Where? Why?

1. In what country was John Paul Jones born?

    _____

2. What did John's father do for a living?

    _____

3. What was John's rank in the navy?

    _____

4. What country donated John's ship?

    _____

5. What did John rename his ship?

    _____

6. What were the words that John reportedly shouted during a battle with a British warship?

    _____

7. What ship did John and his crew capture on September 23, 1779?

    _____

8. What happened to John's ship after the September 23 battle?

    _____

9. In honor of what person did John Paul name his ship?

    _____

10. Where is he buried?

    _____

11. What was John's real name?

    _____

12. Why did John leave Scotland?

    _____

Independence Battle Rap

Setting the Stage

Common Sense, a pamphlet written by Thomas Paine, was published in January 1776. Read by probably half of the colonists, it convinced many that a revolution for independence was needed.

The melody of *Yankee Doodle* was borrowed from a very old song, possibly from an old children's game. The words, *yankee doodle,* meant a dishonest fool. Using the tune, British soldiers sang numerous, made-up verses mocking the Colonial militia during the early revolutionary years. However, the song came back to haunt the Redcoats as they retreated from battles at Lexington and Concord. Patriots taunted them by whistling and singing their own newly created, satirical verses of *Yankee Doodle.* Sung throughout the Revolutionary War, it represented the spirit of the colonial people.

Ready to fight at a minute's notice, the Minutemen were made up of farmers and townspeople. The first battles of the Revolutionary War occurred at Lexington and Concord. British troops greatly outnumbered the Patriots at Lexington, but the Redcoats were surprised by the Minutemen at the Old North Bridge near Concord.

Early battles were fought in the northern colonies. The Green Mountain Boys, led by Ethan Allen, captured Fort Ticonderoga. In the Battle of Bunker Hill, actually Breed's Hill, the British won the Hill but suffered heavy losses. The Colonial militia retreated only when their ammunition ran out.

Long Island, Harlem Heights, Fort Washington—these battles in late 1776 eventually led to the control of New York City by the British. On September 21, 1776, the city burned, but the British occupied it for the next seven years.

General Washington crossed the Delaware River to avoid defeat in the winter of 1776. On Christmas night he moved his troops back across the river. Redcoats were surprised at Trenton, and the Patriots followed the victory with the capture of Princeton.

In October 1777, a victory by the Continental forces at Saratoga was considered a turning point. Several thousand British troops surrendered, and France became convinced that the colonies could win the war. France later supported the Patriot cause by sending money, supplies, soldiers, and its naval fleet.

Washington's troops spent the bitter winter of 1777–1778 at Valley Forge but emerged with renewed spirit. The last major battle in the northern colonies was in June 1778 at Monmouth, New Jersey.

One of America's greatest naval victories occurred on September 23, 1779, when Captain John Paul Jones defeated the powerful British warship, *Serapis.* A hand-to-hand battle took place after Jones rammed his *Bonhomme Richard* into the British vessel.

From *13 Colonies! 13 Years! Integrating Content Standards and the Arts to Teach the American Revolution.* By Mary Wheeler and Jill Terlep. Music by Mary Wheeler. Illustrations by Jill Terlep. Westport, CT: Libraries Unlimited/Teacher Ideas Press. Copyright © 2006.

Southern campaigns were fought during 1779–1781 at Savannah, Charleston, and Cowpens as the momentum began to swing toward the Patriots. Cornwallis's troops surrendered to General Washington and the Continental Army on October 19, 1781, at Yorktown.

Independence Battle Rap

Common sense, common sense,
The Independence War.
Common sense, the Yankee Doodles fought for freedom evermore.

Lexington then Concord, that's where the war began.
"Got my musket, I am ready!" called the Minuteman.

Green Mountain Boys went marching up north to Lake Champlain.
The Patriots stormed the fort at dawn in a surprise campaign.

Common sense, common sense,
The Independence War.
Common sense, the Yankee Doodles fought for freedom evermore.

Redcoats met the Patriots, who battled hard, but still
With ammunition running low, they lost at Bunker Hill.

The New York City battles for our troops did not go well.
The year was 1776, but still too soon to tell.

Common sense, common sense,
The Independence War.
Common sense, the Yankee Doodles fought for freedom evermore.

On Christmas night George took his men across the Delaware.
At Princeton and at Trenton, he attacked the British there.

The Saratoga victory was led by General Gates.
This turning point in '77 helped seal our nation's fate.

Common sense, common sense,
The Independence War.
Common sense, the Yankee Doodles fought for freedom evermore.

Disease and awful weather plagued the Patriots, but George
Continued in the winter to have hope at Valley Forge.

Onward to the south they charged and 1781
Brought victory at Yorktown, and our country had begun!

Common sense, common sense,
The Independence War.
Common sense, the Yankee Doodles fought for freedom evermore.

From *13 Colonies! 13 Years! Integrating Content Standards and the Arts to Teach the American Revolution.* By Mary Wheeler and Jill Terlep. Music by Mary Wheeler. Illustrations by Jill Terlep. Westport, CT: Libraries Unlimited/Teacher Ideas Press. Copyright © 2006.

NAME_____ DATE_____

Independence Battle Rap

List 10 Revolutionary War battle sites.

1. _____   6. _____

2. _____   7. _____

3. _____   8. _____

4. _____   9. _____

5. _____   10._____

How has your life been affected by the sacrifices of the men and women who served in those battles?

_____

_____

_____

_____

_____

_____

_____

_____

_____

_____

_____

_____

_____

_____

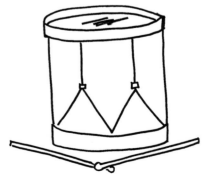

From *13 Colonies! 13 Years! Integrating Content Standards and the Arts to Teach the American Revolution.* By Mary Wheeler and Jill Terlep. Music by Mary Wheeler. Illustrations by Jill Terlep. Westport, CT: Libraries Unlimited/Teacher Ideas Press. Copyright © 2006.

Wisdom Is Higher
A Tribute to Phillis Wheatley

Setting the Stage

Born in West Africa, Phillis Wheatley came to the colonies on a slave ship in 1761. She was purchased in Boston by Mr. and Mrs. John Wheatley, who raised her like a daughter.

Phillis was exceptionally intelligent and soon learned to read and write. She studied the Bible and English poetry, and she began expressing her own thoughts about religion, freedom, and slavery. Phillis also wrote about colonial affairs. Because he was impressed with her work, George Washington invited her to speak at Cambridge, Massachusetts. Her poems were published both in the colonies and in Britain.

In 1773, Phillis was presented to Lady Huntingdon, Lord Dartmouth, and other distinguished people in London. Before being presented to George III, she returned home quickly upon learning of the poor health of her mistress. Following the deaths of the Wheatleys, Phillis was set free, but she was utterly destitute. She married an unworthy man and bore three babies who did not survive childhood. Phillis died in poverty in December 1784. Her contributions to the world were not only her poems, but also the manner in which she lived.

"Wisdom is higher than a fool can reach." is a sentence from Phillis's poem, "On Virtue." That line was used in the both the title and words of this song.

Wisdom Is Higher

Who sailed? Who sailed?
Who sailed the ship across the sea?
He could bind
The chains around her legs,
But he could not restrain her mind.

Who sailed? Who sailed?
Who sailed the ship across the sea?
Away she climbed
With pen . . . and books for steps,
And so she left his chains behind.

"Wisdom is higher than a fool can reach.
Wisdom is higher than a fool can reach."
Higher, higher, higher, higher—
"Wisdom is higher than a fool can reach."

Wisdom Is Higher

A Tribute to Phillis Wheatley

Phillis Wheatley came to the United States on a slave ship more than 200 years ago. Write a letter to her. Describe the changes that have occurred in our country since the American Revolution. (Include the five parts of a friendly letter.)

(Heading) _____

_____

_____ *(Greeting)*

(Body) _____

_____

_____

_____

_____

_____

_____

_____

_____

(Closing) _____

(Signature) _____

Powder Your Wigs

Setting the Stage

Skilled craftsmen produced many kinds of goods during colonial times. Conestoga wagons, designed to be pulled over rugged trails, were built by wainwrights in Pennsylvania. Gunsmiths made Kentucky rifles, whose accuracy and easy loading made them very popular with woodsmen. Snuffboxes, which were considered status symbols, were sometimes even created from silver by silversmiths.

Imitating the English custom, many men wore wigs. The hairpieces were made and dressed by wigmakers and barbers. Some gentlemen, like George Washington, powdered their own hair to look like wigs. Sewn by the hatters, the three-cornered hats were popular because they fit under men's arms when they didn't want to muss their wigs.

Many artisans wore leather aprons because the apparel was tough and protective. Carpenters, shoemakers, silversmiths, blacksmiths, candlemakers—all such men were called *leather aprons* because they wore them on the job.

Practicing their trades in colonial times were bookbinders, potters, silversmiths, braziers, coopers, millers, wainwrights, chandlers, sawyers, and bakers. Often using compulsory or voluntary apprentices, many of the craftsmen worked with great skill. These artisans and many others laid the groundwork for American industry.

During the war, many colonial women managed the households while their husbands were away. A lot of wives worked the farms while others ran the businesses. Some women accompanied their husbands to the battlefields where they cooked, carried water, or helped in other ways.

Most African Americans were slaves. In the North, however, a few thousand African Americans earned their livings as seamen, craftsmen, businesspeople, or in other professions.

Powder Your Wigs

From the Conestoga wagons to the old Kentucky rifles
And the fancy silver snuffboxes they made,
The cooper and the fuller and all those other artisans
Were very, very skillful at their trades.

So - o - o - o
X - X - X - X - X - X - X - X*
Powder your wigs and tip your hats to the craftsmen long ago.
What kinds of jobs did they once do? That's what we'd like to show.

X - X - X - X - X - X - X - X
Slash the sword the cutler made; be careful of the sharpened blade.

A locksmith works with grooves and keys, so tumble like his locks do, please.

Help the wainwright earn a meal; go in circles like his wheel.

Fold your middle like the sheets that the bookbinder completes.

Like the chandler, stir the pot. Make the candles; ouch, it's hot!

Ride to town and back, of course, when the blacksmith shoes your horse.

Make a windmill, do not strain. The miller needs to grind the grain.

Sawyers always work in pairs; saw the logs for all the stairs.

Sift the flour and knead the dough. The baker says, "Come on, let's go."

Fire the cannon, ring the bell! The brazier has some bronze to sell.

Tap your boots on down the street; the cobbler makes some happy feet.

X - X - X - X - X - X - X - X
Powder your wigs and tip your hats to the craftsmen long ago.
What kinds of jobs did they once do? That's what we tried to show.

*Clap or snap fingers on the Xs.

From *13 Colonies! 13 Years! Integrating Content Standards and the Arts to Teach the American Revolution*. By Mary Wheeler and Jill Terlep. Music by Mary Wheeler. Illustrations by Jill Terlep. Westport, CT: Libraries Unlimited/Teacher Ideas Press. Copyright © 2006.

Powder Your Wigs

Choose any of the colonial occupations listed in the song, and pretend you work on that job. Write a conversation that you might have with a customer. Use proper punctuation marks, and don't forget to indent each time you change speakers.

_____

_____

_____

_____

_____

_____

_____

_____

_____

_____

_____

_____

_____

_____

_____

_____

Constitutional Convention

Setting the Stage

The Articles of Confederation was a "firm league of friendship," but it did not provide a strong enough national government. Therefore, in 1787 the Second Continental Congress asked each state to send delegates to the Constitutional Convention in Philadelphia. Between May 25 and September 17, a new frame of government was created.

George Washington was chosen as president at the Grand Convention. Among the delegates were Benjamin Franklin (oldest signer), Alexander Hamilton (first secretary of the treasury), Gouverneur Morris (drafter of the document), and James Madison (referred to as Father of the Constitution).

To encourage a free exchange of ideas, deliberations were kept secret. However, notes written by James Madison and others provide information of some convention activities. The Virginia Plan called for a strong national government, "consisting of a *SUPREME* Legislative, Executive, and Judiciary." Paterson of New Jersey introduced a proposal, which gave equal power to small states. A conflict about representation occurred between states with large and small populations. According to the Connecticut Compromise, membership would be based on population in one house and equal state vote in the other.

The Convention designated the Constitution as the "Supreme Law of the Land." With the words "We the People," authority to rule the United States was placed upon its citizens.

Constitutional Convention

Constitutional Convention! Constitutional Convention!
To Madison and Washington
And delegates from all those states
We thank you
For going to
The Constitutional Convention.

Said Madison to Washington, "We want you to preside.
These Articles don't work although our 13 states have tried.
We need a Constitution and our country unified."
"I'll lead this Grand Convention, then," George Washington replied.

Constitutional Convention! Constitutional Convention!
To Madison and Washington
And delegates from all those states
We thank you
For going to
The Constitutional Convention.

Said Madison to Washington, "The Connecticut Compromise
Ensures each state an equal vote, regardless of its size."

"Two houses," answered Washington, "who make our laws is wise.
This governmental framework is the best we can devise."

Constitutional Convention! Constitutional Convention!
To Madison and Washington
And delegates from all those states
We thank you
For going to
The Constitutional Convention.
THANK YOU!

NAME _____ DATE _____

Constitutional Convention

Who? What? When? Where? Why?

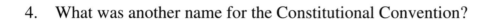

1. Where was the Constitutional Convention held?

    _____

2. When did the Convention take place?

    _____

3. Who was chosen as the president of the Convention?

    _____

4. What was another name for the Constitutional Convention?

    _____

5. Who was the oldest signer of the Constitution?

    _____

6. Who was the first secretary of the treasury?

    _____

7. Who is called the "Father of the Constitution"?

    _____

8. Who kept notes about Convention activities?

    _____

9. Who introduced a proposal to give equal power to smaller states?

    _____

10. What agreement guaranteed that one house would be based on population and the other on equal states?

    _____

11. Why should we thank the delegates from all the states for going to the Constitutional Convention? Write about it on another sheet of paper.

From *13 Colonies! 13 Years! Integrating Content Standards and the Arts to Teach the American Revolution.* By Mary Wheeler and Jill Terlep. Music by Mary Wheeler. Illustrations by Jill Terlep. Westport, CT: Libraries Unlimited/Teacher Ideas Press. Copyright © 2006.

Sing in a Circle

Setting the Stage

The bald eagle was chosen as our country's national emblem on June 10, 1782. Its majestic looks, great strength, and long life influenced its selection as the symbol of the United States. Representing unlimited freedom, the eagle lives atop mountains and soars through valleys and spaces above.

Benjamin Franklin was opposed to picking the eagle for the symbol, and he wrote, "he is a bird of bad moral character … too lazy to fish … and a rank coward." Franklin believed the turkey was a "much more respectable bird."

A story told about one of the first battles of the Revolution recounts how the morning noises of the fighting awoke the sleeping eagles. Circling the fighting men, the Patriots claimed the birds were shrieking for freedom.

The need for an official seal was determined at the Second Continental Congress, but it was not until 1787 that Congress officially adopted the American bald eagle as the national emblem. The Great Seal depicts an eagle, facing front, with wings spread, holding an olive branch in his right talon and a bundle of 13 arrows in his left. The Latin phrase "E Pluribus Unum" is inscribed on a scroll held in his beak. These words represented the unification of the colonies as a country and are translated as, "Out of many, one."

Sing in a Circle

Our country has many colors. Each person has a view,
But the voice of our America is always red, white, and blue.
Come, let's sing in a circle. See our eagle soar.
Come, let's sing in a circle. Freedom evermore!

Our people have disagreements, but we're united throughout the land
That the strength of our America is the liberty for which we stand.
Come, let's sing in a circle. See our eagle soar.
Come, let's sing in a circle. Freedom evermore!

We say what we believe in. We fear not another day.
We give thanks for our America and for livin' in the USA.
Come, let's sing in a circle. See our eagle soar.
Come, let's sing in a circle. Freedom evermore!

From *13 Colonies! 13 Years! Integrating Content Standards and the Arts to Teach the American Revolution.* By Mary Wheeler and Jill Terlep. Music by Mary Wheeler. Illustrations by Jill Terlep. Westport, CT: Libraries Unlimited/Teacher Ideas Press. Copyright © 2006.

NAME _____ DATE _____

Sing in a Circle

Draw a patriotic picture. Write a caption beneath the drawing. You may draw an eagle, copy the official seal, illustrate a line from the song, or choose another scene to portray your patriotic ideas.

Colonial Terms—Vocabulary

ancestor—one from whom a person is descended

apprentice—a person learning a skill while working for an experienced person

artisan—a craftsperson

Bonhomme Richard—Continental naval ship; refitted, aging, French merchant ship that was renamed by John Paul Jones in honor of Benjamin Franklin

boycott—when a group refuses to buy certain products as a way of protesting

cannon—a large, heavy gun usually mounted on a carriage

checks and balances—a system of separating government so each part keeps the others from taking too much power

colony—a settlement ruled by a distant country

Conestoga wagon—a broad-wheeled, covered wagon usually drawn by six horses and used especially for transporting freight across the prairies

declaration—something a person or a group writes or speaks to make a position clear; a statement

delegate—a person chosen to represent a group of people

executive branch—the president and his staff; the branch of government charged with implementing and administering the law

forefather—a person of an earlier period and common heritage

inauguration—a formal ceremony at which a government official, particularly the president, is sworn into office

independence—not subject to control by others; self-governing

judicial branch—the U.S. Supreme Court; the part of government charged with resolving disputes

legal tender—money that is legally valid for the payment of debts and must be accepted for that purpose when offered

legislative branch—the Senate and the House of Representatives (together known as Congress); the part of government charged with making laws

Liberty Bell—patriotic symbol of the country that has the following biblical words inscribed on it: "Proclaim liberty throughout the land unto all the inhabitants thereof."

Loyalist—a colonist who supported England

militia—an army made up of ordinary citizens

musket—a shoulder gun carried by infantry

Parliament—Britain's lawmaking body

Poor Richard's Almanack—a collection of witty and wise short sayings, calendars, and miscellaneous information published annually by Benjamin Franklin

rammer staff—a device used to stuff ammunition into a cannon

Serapis—British warship captured by John Paul Jones on September 23, 1779

snuffbox—a small box used for holding snuff (a preparation of pulverized tobacco to be inhaled through the nostrils, chewed, or placed against the gums) usually carried on the person

tariff—a tax charged on goods brought into a country

tax—money people give the government to help pay for the services it provides to them

Yankee Doodle—unflattering British nickname for American colonial militia

From *13 Colonies! 13 Years! Integrating Content Standards and the Arts to Teach the American Revolution.* By Mary Wheeler and Jill Terlep. Music by Mary Wheeler. Illustrations by Jill Terlep. Westport, CT: Libraries Unlimited/Teacher Ideas Press. Copyright © 2006.

Colonial Terms Crossword Puzzle

tax	legal tender	militia	artisan
colony	independence	*Bonhomme Richard*	Conestoga wagon
boycott	tariff	declaration	ancestor
cannon			

ACROSS

3. Not subject to control by others

7. A broad-wheeled, covered wagon

8. Money that is legally valid

12. A craftsperson

13. One from whom a person is descended

DOWN

1. An army made up of ordinary citizens

2. When a group refuses to buy certain products as a way of protesting

4. A settlement ruled by a distant country

5. A statement to make a position clear

6. The Continental naval ship captained by John Paul Jones

9. Money people give the government to help pay for services it provides

10. A large, heavy gun

11. A tax charged on goods brought into a country

From *13 Colonies! 13 Years! Integrating Content Standards and the Arts to Teach the American Revolution.* By Mary Wheeler and Jill Terlep. Music by Mary Wheeler. Illustrations by Jill Terlep. Westport, CT: Libraries Unlimited/Teacher Ideas Press. Copyright © 2006.

NAME _____ DATE _____

Separate, but Equal

The Constitution separates our federal government into three branches, and a system of **checks and balances** prevents any one branch from becoming too powerful.

Label each branch: **Congress, President, or Supreme Court.**

(Example: Congress)
_____   _____   _____

LEGISLATIVE BRANCH	EXECUTIVE BRANCH	JUDICIAL BRANCH

Match the powers with the correct branch of government, and write them in the appropriate columns.

Carries out the laws   Decides legal cases
Conducts relations with other countries Manages the government
Makes the laws   Approves appointments
Is commander-in-chief   Can declare war
Decides whether laws are constitutional Decides cases between states
Explains the meaning of treaties   Approves treaties

What would happen if one branch of the government became too powerful?

_____

_____

_____

_____

_____

What Does It Mean?

Match the word or term with the correct meaning.

independence	boycott	ancestor
inauguration	militia	checks and balances
declaration	cannon	*Poor Richard's Almanack*
tax		

1. Not subject to control by others; self-governing

    _____

2. One from whom a person is descended

    _____

3. An army made up of ordinary citizens

    _____

4. Money people give the government to help pay for services it provides them

    _____

5. Something a person or a group writes or speaks to make a position clear

    _____

6. A formal ceremony at which a governmental official is sworn into office

    _____

7. A large, heavy gun usually mounted on a carriage

    _____

8. When a group refuses to buy certain products as a way of protesting

    _____

9. System of separating government so each part keeps the others from taking too much power

    _____

10. Published annually by Benjamin Franklin

    _____

From *13 Colonies! 13 Years! Integrating Content Standards and the Arts to Teach the American Revolution.* By Mary Wheeler and Jill Terlep. Music by Mary Wheeler. Illustrations by Jill Terlep. Westport, CT: Libraries Unlimited/Teacher Ideas Press. Copyright © 2006.

Write the letter of the correct word or term with its matching definition.

A. artisan
B. legal tender
C. Liberty Bell
D. forefather
E. colony
F. Parliament
G. musket
H. delegate
I. *Bonhomme Richard*
J. tariff

11. A person of an earlier period and common heritage   _____

12. A shoulder gun carried by infantry   _____

13. A patriotic symbol of the country   _____

14. A person chosen to represent a group of people   _____

15. Money that is legally valid for the payment of debts   _____

16. A settlement ruled by a distant country   _____

17. A continental naval ship captained by John Paul Jones   _____

18. A craftsperson   _____

19. A tax charged on goods brought into a country   _____

20. Britain's lawmaking body   _____

Write sentences using five words from either list. Underline the words you have chosen.

_____

_____

_____

_____

_____

_____

_____

_____

_____

Revolutionary Figures—Vocabulary

Crispus Attucks

Adams, Abigail—(1744–1818) wife of John Adams; noted letter writer

Adams, John—(1735–1826) second president of the United States, 1797–1801; one of the Founding Fathers of the new nation

Allen, Ethan—(1738–1789) led Green Mountain Boys in early battles fought in the northern colonies

Attucks, Crispus—(1723–1770) African American, former slave; killed during the Boston Massacre, March 5, 1770

Committee of Correspondence—the group formed to watch and report British activities to the colonists

Cornwallis, Charles—(1728–1805) English general in Revolutionary War; surrendered to Americans in 1871

Franklin, Benjamin—(1706–1790) printer, writer, publisher, scientist, and inventor; delegate to the Constitutional Convention

Green Mountain Boys—group of fighters, led by Ethan Allen, who seized Ft. Ticonderoga

Hamilton, Alexander—(1755–1804) delegate to the Constitutional Convention; first secretary of the treasury

Hays, Molly (Pitcher)—(1754–1832) artillery wife who shared the rigors of war at the Battle of Monmouth with her husband

Henry, Patrick—(1736–1799) revolutionary leader and orator

Jefferson, Thomas—(1743–1826) third president of the United States, 1801–1809; one of the Founding Fathers of the new nation

Jones, John Paul—(1747–1792) heroic naval officer who commanded the ship *Bonhomme Richard*

King George III—(1760–1820) king of England; supported policies that led to the American Revolution

Loyalist—any colonist who supported the British

Madison, James—(1751–1836) "Father of the Constitution"; fourth president of the United States, 1809–1817

Minuteman—a member of the American colonial militia who was prepared to fight at a minute's notice

Morris, Gouverneur—(1752–1816) a member of the Continental Congress

Paine, Thomas—(1737–1809) wrote *Common Sense*, urging a declaration of independence

Patriot—any American colonist who opposed the British

Redcoat—a member of the British army

Revere, Paul—(1735–1818) rode from Boston to Lexington, April 18, 1775, warning colonists along the way of a British march

Shay, Daniel—(1747–1825) led rebellion in 1787 that helped convince many Americans that a stronger national government was needed

Sons of Liberty—the group of colonists opposed to British control; responsible for the Boston Tea Party; formed in Boston, encouraged colonists to defy the Stamp Act

Washington, George—(1723–1799) commanded continental armies during the Revolution; first president of the United States, 1789–1797

Wheatley, Phillis—(1753–1784) African American poet

Abigail Adams

Revolutionary Figures Crossword Puzzle

Patriot
Sons of Liberty
Redcoat
Molly Hays
Minuteman
Patrick Henry

Daniel Shay
King George (III)
John Adams
Ethan Allen
Thomas Jefferson

Paul Revere
Committee of Correspondence
Loyalist
Ben Franklin
Patriot

ACROSS

3. Third president of the United States

4. Artillery wife at the Battle of Monmouth

6. Any colonist who opposed the British

7. Led the Green Mountain Boys

9. King of England

10. Any colonist who supported England

12. A member of the British army

13. Printer, writer, publisher, scientist, inventor, statesman

14. Warned colonists of British march on April 18, 1775

15. A soldier prepared to fight in a minute

DOWN

1. Group formed to report British activities to the colonists
2. Second president of the United States
5. Group of men opposed to British control
8. Led rebellion in 1787 that convinced Americans of the need for a stronger government
11. Revolutionary leader and orator

NAME _____ DATE _____

Revolutionary Figures

Subtract each problem. Match the answer with the years of each of the American Revolution characters. Write the letter of your answer and the life span in years.

Crispus Attucks

A.　1790
　　−1706

B.　1826
　　−1735

C.　1820
　　−1760

D.　1792
　　−1747

E.　1836
　　−1751

F.　1799
　　−1723

G.　1825
　　−1747

H.　1784
　　−1753

I.　1770
　　−1723

J.　1818
　　−1744
　　　74

K.　1805
　　−1728

L.　1789
　　−1738

M.　1804
　　−1755

N.　1809
　　−1737

O.　1826
　　−1743

P.　1799
　　−1736

1.　Abigail Adams　　　74 yrs.　　　_J_　　　(1744–1818)

2.　John Adams　　　91 yrs.　　　___　　　(　　　)

3.　Ethan Allen　　　51 yrs.　　　___　　　(　　　)

4.　Crispus Attucks　　　47 yrs.　　　___　　　(　　　)

5.　Charles Cornwallis　　　77 yrs.　　　___　　　(　　　)

6.　Benjamin Franklin　　　84 yrs.　　　___　　　(　　　)

7.　Alexander Hamilton　　　49 yrs.　　　___　　　(　　　)

8.　Patrick Henry　　　63 yrs.　　　___　　　(　　　)

9.　Thomas Jefferson　　　83 yrs.　　　___　　　(　　　)

10.　John Paul Jones　　　45 yrs.　　　___　　　(　　　)

11.　King George III　　　60 yrs.　　　___　　　(　　　)

12.　James Madison　　　85 yrs.　　　___　　　(　　　)

13.　Thomas Paine　　　72 yrs.　　　___　　　(　　　)

14.　Daniel Shay　　　78 yrs.　　　___　　　(　　　)

15.　George Washington　　　76 yrs.　　　___　　　(　　　)

16.　Phillis Wheatley　　　31 yrs.　　　___　　　(　　　)

Bonus: What was the average life span of these people? _____

From *13 Colonies! 13 Years! Integrating Content Standards and the Arts to Teach the American Revolution.* By Mary Wheeler and Jill Terlep. Music by Mary Wheeler. Illustrations by Jill Terlep. Westport, CT: Libraries Unlimited/Teacher Ideas Press. Copyright © 2006.

NAME _____ DATE _____

George Washington Was the Best President

A **fact** is something that can be proved true or false. An **opinion** tells a person's ideas or feelings. It cannot be proved true or false. Read these statements about George Washington. Write *fact* or *opinion*.

George Washington ...

1. was the best president of the United States.   _____

2. was the first president of the United States.   _____

3. owned a home in Mt. Vernon, Virginia.   _____

4. married Martha Dandridge Custis on January 6, 1759.   _____

5. was the greatest military leader in our country's history. _____

6. commanded the Revolutionary Army.   _____

7. felt sad about leaving his family to go to war.   _____

8. attended the Constitutional Convention.   _____

9. liked all of the members of the Second Continental Congress. _____

10. wintered with his troops at Valley Forge, Pennsylvania, in 1777–1778. _____

11. believed General Cornwallis of Britain was an excellent soldier. _____

12. was inaugurated as president of the United States April 30, 1789. _____

13. was the son of Augustine and Mary Ball Washington.   _____

From *13 Colonies! 13 Years! Integrating Content Standards and the Arts to Teach the American Revolution.* By Mary Wheeler and Jill Terlep. Music by Mary Wheeler. Illustrations by Jill Terlep. Westport, CT: Libraries Unlimited/Teacher Ideas Press. Copyright © 2006.

Occupations of the Era— Vocabulary

apothecary—mixed medicines

baker—prepared food by baking it

barber—shaved heads and faces, pulled teeth, let blood, and made wigs

bell founder—made metal bells

blacksmith—forged iron, shod horses and oxen, and was an expert in diseases of animals

blockprinter—made wallpaper with prints on it

bookbinder—bound books

brazier—worked with brass

cabinetmaker—made cabinets, chairs, furniture of wood

carpenter—built or repaired structures or their structural parts

chandler—made candles

clockmaker—made or fixed clocks

cobbler—mended or made shoes and often other leather goods

cooper—made or repaired wooden casks or tubs

cutler—made, dealt in, or repaired edged or cutting tools, specifically for cutting and eating food (called cutlery)

fuller—prepared woolen cloth by cleaning and thumping it

gunsmith—made guns

hatter—made, sold, or cleaned and repaired hats

hornsmith—prepared animal horns so they could be made into useful items, such as gun powder carriers and spectacle frames

housewright—framed a house

itinerant—moved from farm to farm doing various jobs, as needed

leather apron—craftsperson who wore a leather apron, and thus was nicknamed leather apron

locksmith—made or repaired locks

miller—ground grain into flour

plumber—worked with lead, making bullets and pipes

potter—made pottery

sawyer—sawed logs

shoemaker—made or repaired shoes

silversmith—made articles of silver

tailor—stitched breeches, long coats, cloaks, and capes

tanner—tanned the hides into leather

tinker—mended metal household objects like dipper handles, pewter plates or bowls, and basins

tobacconist—made snuff, chewing, or pipe tobacco

wainwright—made and repaired wagons

Occupations of the Era Crossword Puzzle

hatter	wainwright	clockmaker	potter
bookbinder	leather apron	bellfounder	locksmith
baker	brazier	cutler	sawyer
carpenter	miller	shoemaker	cooper

ACROSS

2. Reference to craftspeople who wore leather aprons
4. One who makes and repairs wagons
6. One who makes, sells, or repairs hats
8. One who makes or repairs tools for cutting food
10. One who saws
13. One who binds books
14. One who works with brass

DOWN

1. One who makes or repairs locks
3. One who makes pottery
5. One who makes or repairs shoes
7. One who makes metal bells
8. One who makes or fixes clocks
9. One who builds or repairs structures
11. One who makes or repairs wooden casks or tubs
12. One who grinds grain into flour
14. One who prepares food by baking it

NAME _____ DATE _____

Two Left Feet

Did you know that during the colonial days there was no such thing as a left and right shoe? Both were made the same. Soldiers in the American Revolution were even encouraged to keep interchanging their two shoes so they would not form to their feet. Then, if the soldier was killed, another person could use his shoes.

A shoemaker was one of the skilled artisans, and there were many more. Choose one of the occupations from the *Occupations of the Era—Vocabulary*, and learn more about it. What kind of tools, materials, and equipment were needed to perform the job? Where could you find this worker—in a town, city, countryside, by the sea …? How was he paid? Did he wear a leather apron? Write a report about your findings. At the end of your report, decide whether you would have liked to do that job if you had lived in the Revolutionary times. Include that decision in your conclusion and give reasons. List the sources that you used.

Occupation Selected: _____

Sources:

_____

_____

_____

_____

_____

_____

_____

_____

_____

_____

_____

_____

_____

From *13 Colonies! 13 Years! Integrating Content Standards and the Arts to Teach the American Revolution.* By Mary Wheeler and Jill Terlep. Music by Mary Wheeler. Illustrations by Jill Terlep. Westport, CT: Libraries Unlimited/Teacher Ideas Press. Copyright © 2006.

NAME _____ DATE _____

I Need Help. Whom Shall I Call?

Write the name of the artisan in the blanks. Here are my needs:

1. _____ shoes for Bessie the horse

2. _____ rain barrel to catch some water

3. _____ new cloak for winter

4. _____ flour for baking bread

5. _____ new wheels for the Conestoga wagon

6. _____ wallpaper for the fancy new dining room

7. _____ carrier for gunpowder

8. _____ bell for the new community church

9. _____ Uncle John's tooth pulled

10. _____ candles

From the *Occupations of the Era* list, choose the **three** most important artisans in the community (rank them in order), and explain your reasons for selecting them.

1. _____ Reason:_____
   (artisan)

   _____

   _____

2. _____ Reason:_____

   _____

   _____

3. _____ Reason:_____

   _____

   _____

From *13 Colonies! 13 Years! Integrating Content Standards and the Arts to Teach the American Revolution.* By Mary Wheeler and Jill Terlep. Music by Mary Wheeler. Illustrations by Jill Terlep. Westport, CT: Libraries Unlimited/Teacher Ideas Press. Copyright © 2006.

Match the craftsman with the job.   Write the matching letter in the blank.

A. brazier   B. apothecary   C. bookbinder   D. locksmith
E. fuller   F. cutler   G. silversmith   H. cobbler
I. plumber   J. tinker   K. housewright   L. baker

11. _____   mixed medicines

12. _____   prepared food by baking it

13. _____   made or repaired locks

14. _____   mended or made shoes and often other leather goods

15. _____   made, dealt in, or repaired edged or cutting tools, specifically for cutting and eating food

16. _____   mended metal household objects such as dipper handles, pewter plates or bowls, and basins

17. _____   made articles of silver

18. _____   worked with lead, making bullets and pipes

19. _____   worked with brass

20. _____   bound books

Choose four artisans from the above list and use their names in a sentence. Underline the words you chose.

_____

_____

_____

_____

_____

_____

_____

From *13 Colonies! 13 Years! Integrating Content Standards and the Arts to Teach the American Revolution*. By Mary Wheeler and Jill Terlep. Music by Mary Wheeler. Illustrations by Jill Terlep. Westport, CT: Libraries Unlimited/Teacher Ideas Press. Copyright © 2006.

Events and Documents— Vocabulary

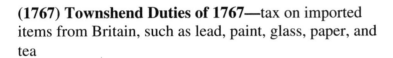

(1763) Proclamation of 1763—British proclamation forbidding colonists from moving west of the Appalachian Mountains

(1765) Stamp Act of 1765—passed by Parliament, required an official stamp (paid as a tax) on almost everything printed on paper

(1767) Townshend Duties of 1767—tax on imported items from Britain, such as lead, paint, glass, paper, and tea

(1770) Boston Massacre—March 5, 1770, colonists taunted British soldiers who fired at the group of defenseless protesters

(1773) Boston Tea Party—December 16, 1773, Patriots, dressed as Indians, threw tea from British ships in Boston Harbor as protest

(1774) Intolerable Acts—passed by Parliament in 1774 to punish Americans for the Boston Tea Party; ended town meetings, removed some power from the Massachusetts Assembly, closed Boston port, imposed quartering of British troops (called the Coercive Acts in England)

(1774) First Continental Congress—Philadelphia, 1774, members drew up list of complaints against King George III and Parliament

(1775) Second Continental Congress—Philadelphia, 1775, members wrote the *Articles of Confederation* and agreed to support the colonists

(1775) Battle of Lexington—April 19, 1775, the Revolutionary War began when Patriots, warned by Paul Revere, met British General Thomas Gage at Lexington, Massachusetts

(1775) Battle of Bunker Hill—Americans lost Breed's Hill (Boston) to the British, who suffered heavy losses

From *13 Colonies! 13 Years! Integrating Content Standards and the Arts to Teach the American Revolution.* By Mary Wheeler and Jill Terlep. Music by Mary Wheeler. Illustrations by Jill Terlep. Westport, CT: Libraries Unlimited/Teacher Ideas Press. Copyright © 2006.

(1776) *Common Sense*—pamphlet written by Thomas Paine, January 1776, argued for colonial independence

(1776) Declaration of Independence—document written by Thomas Jefferson on July 4, 1776, declaring independence from England

(1777) Saratoga Battle—American victory, British General Burgoyne surrendered in what was considered the turning point of the war in favor of the Patriots

(1777–1778) Winter at Valley Forge—Washington "wintered" his troops outside of Philadelphia, Pennsylvania, where they were trained and better prepared for battle

(1779) Naval Victory—*Bonhomme Richard's* Captain John Paul Jones defeated powerful British warship, *Serapis*

(1781) Battle at Yorktown—October 19, 1781, British General Cornwallis surrendered and accepted American independence

(1781) Articles of Confederation—written by Second Continental Congress, a national plan of government that left governmental powers to the states, "a firm league of friendship," effective 1781

(1783) Treaty of Paris—formal document signed with Britain in 1783, ending Revolutionary War and granting the United States independence

(1787) Shay's Rebellion—rebellion in 1787 by Massachusetts farmers, led by Daniel Shay; helped convince many Americans that a stronger national government was needed

(1787) Constitutional Convention—(Grand Convention) May 25–September 17, 1787, Philadelphia, Independence Hall; delegates created a new frame of United States government

(1787) Connecticut Compromise—agreement reached at Constitutional Convention, 1787, stating legislative membership would be based on population in one house and equal state vote in the other

(1787) Constitution of the United States—written at Constitutional Convention in the summer of 1787, "Supreme Law of the Land"

(1789) Presidential Inauguration of George Washington—April 30, 1789, George Washington was inaugurated as the first president of the United States at Federal Hall in New York City

NAME_____ DATE_____

Events and Documents Crossword Puzzle

Intolerable Acts
Boston Tea Party
Proclamation
Treaty of Paris

Stamp Act
Shay's Rebellion
Boston Massacre
Constitution

Declaration of Independence
Second Continental Congress
Townshend Duties
Common Sense

ACROSS

2. Pamphlet written by Thomas Paine

3. 1787 rebellion by Massachusetts farmers

9. 1767 tax on imported items from Britain

11. Formal document ending the Revolutionary War

DOWN

1. July 4, 1776, document declaring independence from England

3. Parliamentary law of 1775 requiring stamps on printed materials

4. Members wrote the Articles of Confederation, 1775

5. British soldiers fired at a group of defenseless protesters

6. Patriots threw tea in Boston Harbor

7. 1774 Acts meant to punish Americans for Boston Tea Party

8. "Supreme Law of the Land"

10. 1763, Britain forbid colonists from moving west of the Appalachian Mountains

From *13 Colonies! 13 Years! Integrating Content Standards and the Arts to Teach the American Revolution.* By Mary Wheeler and Jill Terlep. Music by Mary Wheeler. Illustrations by Jill Terlep. Westport, CT: Libraries Unlimited/Teacher Ideas Press. Copyright © 2006.

"Why Stand We Here Idle?" Let's Act Up!

A. Stamp Act
B. Declaration of Independence
C. Boston Massacre
D. Battle of Bunker Hill
E. First Continental Congress
F. Constitutional Convention
G. Treaty of Paris
H. Townshend Duties
I. Saratoga Battle
J. Connecticut Compromise

K. Winter at Valley Forge
L. Battle at Yorktown
M. Shay's Rebellion
N. Constitution of the United States
O. Intolerable Acts
P. Boston Tea Party
Q. *Common Sense*
R. Articles of Confederation
S. Battle of Lexington
T. Second Continental Congress

Write the event or document and its date.

1. American victory, considered turning point of the war in favor of the Patriots

   _____ Date _____

2. Philadelphia—members drew up list of complaints against Parliament and King George III

   _____ Date _____

3. Passed by Parliament in 1774 to punish Americans for the Boston Tea Party, called Coercive Acts in England

   _____ Date _____

4. Americans lost Breed's Hill to British, who suffered heavy losses

   _____ Date _____

5. Pamphlet, written by Thomas Paine, that argued for colonial independence

   _____ Date _____

6. Philadelphia—members wrote the Articles of Confederation

   _____ Date _____

7. Agreement reached at Constitutional Convention, stating legislative membership would be based on population in one house and equal state vote in the other

   _____ Date _____

8. "Supreme Law of the Land"

   _____ Date _____

From *13 Colonies! 13 Years! Integrating Content Standards and the Arts to Teach the American Revolution.* By Mary Wheeler and Jill Terlep. Music by Mary Wheeler. Illustrations by Jill Terlep. Westport, CT: Libraries Unlimited/Teacher Ideas Press. Copyright © 2006.

9.   Rebellion by Massachusetts farmers that helped convince many Americans a stronger national government was needed

_____ Date _____

10.   A national plan of government that left governmental powers to the States, "a firm league of friendship"

_____ Date _____

Write the letter of the matching Event or Document.

11.   _____   May 25–September 17, 1787

12.   _____   1765

13.   _____   1783

14.   _____   March 5, 1770

15.   _____   December 1778–June 1779

16.   _____   April 19, 1775

17.   _____   October 19, 1781

18.   _____   December 16, 1773

19.   _____   July 4, 1776

20.   _____   1767

The Robinson Tea Chest
Just for fun ... look it up.

60   From *13 Colonies! 13 Years! Integrating Content Standards and the Arts to Teach the American Revolution.* By Mary Wheeler and Jill Terlep. Music by Mary Wheeler. Illustrations by Jill Terlep. Westport, CT: Libraries Unlimited/Teacher Ideas Press. Copyright © 2006.

NAME _____ DATE _____

Don't Just Watch, Participate!

Imagine getting the chance to take part in the formation of America. Study the ***Events and Documents—Vocabulary*** list. Would you want to take part in the Boston Tea Party, the writing of the Declaration of Independence, a specific battle, George Washington's inauguration? It is up to you. Select one item from the list. Write a background on the event. Tell why you want to be a part of that moment in history. Describe what you would do.

Event and date _____

Background _____

_____

_____

_____

_____

_____

Reason for choosing this event _____

_____

_____

_____

_____

_____

On a separate sheet of paper, write what part you would play in this event.

From *13 Colonies! 13 Years! Integrating Content Standards and the Arts to Teach the American Revolution.* By Mary Wheeler and Jill Terlep. Music by Mary Wheeler. Illustrations by Jill Terlep. Westport, CT: Libraries Unlimited/Teacher Ideas Press. Copyright © 2006.

Research and Discovery Activities

NAME _____ DATE _____

Settle Down and Get to Work!

In colonial times, just like today, regional areas were diverse, each offering something different to the local inhabitants. Although most occupations were found in all of the areas, some colonies were better known than others for certain trades.

You would have found an emphasis on the water, with people working as fishermen, shipbuilders, and seafarers in the New England colonies of Massachusetts, Connecticut, Rhode Island, and New Hampshire. There were also many farmers in those locations.

In the South, the populations of Maryland, Virginia, North Carolina, South Carolina, and Georgia relied on cash crops, such as tobacco and rice, grown on big farms and plantations to provide their income.

Although many in the colonies of New York, New Jersey, Pennsylvania, and Delaware were farmers, people also worked in the large cities of New York and Philadelphia as artisans. As large ports, these areas brought career opportunities in trade and commerce, as well.

Given the choice to settle anywhere in the colonies, where would you choose to live? What occupation would you pick? Describe your conditions on the job. What factors influenced your selecting that type of work. If you need to, continue on another piece of paper.

_____

_____

_____

_____

_____

_____

_____

_____

_____

_____

_____

_____

_____

_____

_____

From *13 Colonies! 13 Years! Integrating Content Standards and the Arts to Teach the American Revolution.* By Mary Wheeler and Jill Terlep. Music by Mary Wheeler. Illustrations by Jill Terlep. Westport, CT: Libraries Unlimited/Teacher Ideas Press. Copyright © 2006.

Should Have Dunmore

On November 14, 1775, the earl of Dunmore and royal governor of Virginia issued the following proclamation:

"And I do hereby further declare all indentured Servants, Negroes, or others, (appertaining to Rebels,) free that are able and willing to bear Arms, they joining His MAJESTY'S Troops as soon as may be, for the more speedily reducing this Colony to a proper Sense of their Duty, to His MAJESTY'S Leige Subjects …"

With the promise of emancipation, many African American slaves chose to fight on the Loyalist side.

The Patriots fought for freedom from England's rule, and African Americans fought against them for freedom from enslavement. Compare and contrast.

How were the Patriots' and African Americans' reasons and experiences alike? Compare and list five examples.

_____

_____

_____

_____

_____

_____

_____

How were the Patriots' and African Americans' reasons and experiences different? Contrast and list five examples.

_____

_____

_____

_____

_____

_____

_____

From *13 Colonies! 13 Years! Integrating Content Standards and the Arts to Teach the American Revolution.* By Mary Wheeler and Jill Terlep. Music by Mary Wheeler. Illustrations by Jill Terlep. Westport, CT: Libraries Unlimited/Teacher Ideas Press. Copyright © 2006.

NAME_____ DATE_____

A City of Your Very Own

When the colonists came to North America, their settlements had to be built from scratch. It was hard work clearing the land, felling the trees, and building the structures. The planning that went into those earliest cities is still evident today in the oldest towns of the original colonies.

If you were one of the early planners, how would you lay out a city of your own? Well-rounded towns included businesses, places of worship, schools, government buildings, public spaces like parks and squares, and homes.

Draw your own town map. Lay out the streets, and put in important buildings. Color it and draw buildings in different sizes to show the different structure uses. Use the *Key* to show what the colors mean. Look at the *Occupations of the Era* list for ideas on the businesses to include in your map. You may use a separate piece of paper, if you need more space, or use the box below. Be sure to name your town.

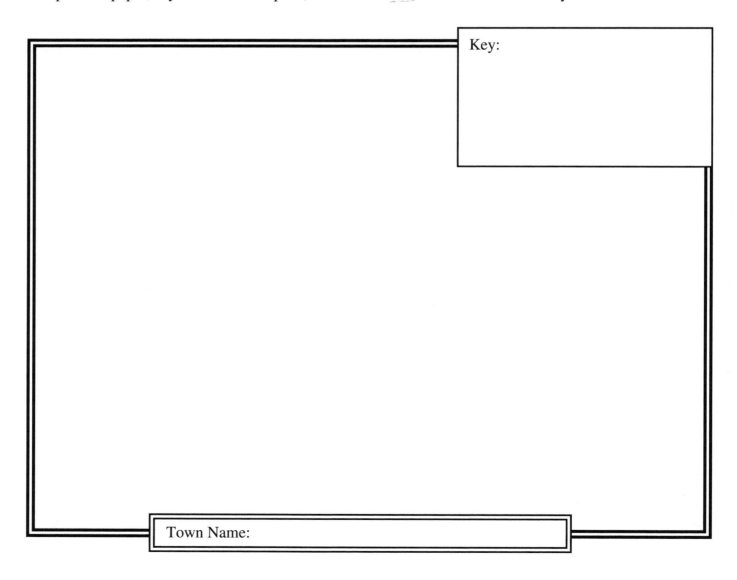

Key:

Town Name:

From *13 Colonies! 13 Years! Integrating Content Standards and the Arts to Teach the American Revolution.* By Mary Wheeler and Jill Terlep. Music by Mary Wheeler. Illustrations by Jill Terlep. Westport, CT: Libraries Unlimited/Teacher Ideas Press. Copyright © 2006.

Whence You Came, Part I

Match the speaker or document with the quotation.

From *Poor Richard's Almanack:*

"Think of three Things—whence you came, where you are going, and to Whom you must account."

Stirring words from the Revolutionary years inspire us yet today, and they must be remembered, repeated, and celebrated by every new generation of Americans.

George Washington, Inaugural Address, April 30, 1789

Patrick Henry, Virginia House of Burgesses Speech

Thomas Paine, *Common Sense*

Preamble to the Constitution of the United States

Declaration of Independence

Abigail Adams, Letter to John Adams, March 31, 1776

Quotes from "whence you came"

1. "The sun never shined on a cause of greater worth. 'Tis not the affair of a city, a county, a province, or a kingdom; but of a continent—of at least one-eighth part of the habitable globe. 'Tis not the concern of a day, a year, or an age; posterity are virtually involved in the contest, and will be more or less affected even to the end of time by the proceedings now. Now is the seedtime of continental union, faith, and honor."

Source:

_____

_____

2. "We the people of the United States, in order to form a more perfect Union, establish justice, insure domestic tranquility, provide for the common defense, promote the general welfare, and secure the blessings of liberty to ourselves and our posterity, do ordain and establish this Constitution for the United States of America."

Source:

_____

_____

3. "We hold these truths to be self-evident, that all men are created equal, that they are endowed by their Creator with certain unalienable Rights, that among these are Life, Liberty and the pursuit of Happiness. That to secure these rights, Governments are instituted among Men, deriving their just powers from the consent of the governed, That whenever any Form of Government becomes destructive of these ends, it is the Right of the People to alter or to abolish it, and to institute new Government, laying its foundation on such principles and organizing its powers in such form, as to them shall seem most likely to effect their Safety and Happiness."

Source:

_____

_____

4. "Gentlemen may cry peace, peace—but there is no peace. The war is actually begun! The next gale that sweeps from the north will bring to our ears the clash of resounding arms! Why stand we here idle? What is it the gentlemen wish? What would they have: Is life so dear, or peace so sweet, as to be purchased at the price of chains and slavery? Forbid it, almighty God! I know not what course others may take; but as for me, give me liberty, or give me death!"

Source:

_____

_____

5. "… the preservation of the sacred fire of liberty and the destiny of the republican model of government are justly considered, perhaps, as 'deeply', as 'finally', staked on the experiment entrusted to the hands of the American people."

Source:

_____

_____

6. "In the new Code of Laws which I suppose it will be necessary for you to make I desire you would Remember the Ladies, and be more generous and favourable to them than your ancestors. Do not put such unlimited powers into the hands of the Husbands. Remember all men would be tyrants if they could. If particular care and attention is not paid to the Ladies, we are determined to forment a Rebellion, and will not hold ourselves bound by any laws in which we have not voice, or Representation."

Source:

_____

_____

Whence You Came, Part II

Choose one of the quotations, and recopy it. Memorize the words.

Selection: _____

_____

_____

_____

_____

_____

_____

_____

_____

_____

_____

_____

_____

_____

_____

_____

NAME _____ DATE _____

Grand Convention (Plus One)

Let's rewrite history. Instead of fifty-five delegates to the Constitutional Convention, there were fifty-six. A well-respected Native American was invited to participate in Philadelphia that summer.

What issue(s) did he address and pursue?

_____
_____
_____
_____
_____
_____
_____

How did his presence affect American history?

_____
_____
_____
_____
_____
_____
_____

What changes would be evident today?

_____
_____
_____
_____
_____
_____
_____

From *13 Colonies! 13 Years! Integrating Content Standards and the Arts to Teach the American Revolution.* By Mary Wheeler and Jill Terlep. Music by Mary Wheeler. Illustrations by Jill Terlep. Westport, CT: Libraries Unlimited/Teacher Ideas Press. Copyright © 2006.

Help from Abroad

The colonies received help from soldiers of other countries during the Revolution. Among them were two officers from Poland, Thaddeus Kosciuszko and Casimir Pulaski. German soldiers, Johann de Kalb and Friedrich von Steuben, and the Marquis de Lafayette from France also served the American cause. Their services were very important to the war effort. Choose a foreign soldier. It can be one of those listed above. Write a report about your findings.

_____

_____

_____

_____

_____

_____

_____

_____

_____

_____

_____

_____

_____

Caimir Pulaski
Some cities celebrate Casimir Pulaski Day. Does yours?

_____

_____

_____

_____

From *13 Colonies! 13 Years! Integrating Content Standards and the Arts to Teach the American Revolution.* By Mary Wheeler and Jill Terlep. Music by Mary Wheeler. Illustrations by Jill Terlep. Westport, CT: Libraries Unlimited/Teacher Ideas Press. Copyright © 2006.

Yankee Doodle

The melody of *Yankee Doodle* was borrowed from a very old song, possibly from an old children's game. The words *yankee doodle* meant a dishonest fool. Using the tune, British soldiers sang numerous, made-up verses mocking the Colonial militia during the early Revolutionary years. However, the song came back to haunt the Redcoats as they retreated from battles at Lexington and C whistling and singing their own newly created, satirical verses of *Yanke Revolutionary War, it represented the spirit of the Colonial people.

Make up a verse of your own for the Patriots.

_____

_____

_____

_____

_____

_____

_____

_____

_____

_____

_____

_____

_____

NAME _____ DATE _____

Just the Facts

Choose any one of the 13 colonies. Draw an outline map of that area. List
13 facts about the chosen colony, and locate 13 sites on your map. Include any sites related to your facts.

Example: Pennsylvania

    1.   Benjamin Franklin lived in Philadelphia.

    2.   Troops wintered at Valley Forge in 1777–1778.

Colony: _____

Facts:

  1. _____

  2. _____

  3. _____

  4. _____

  5. _____

  6. _____

  7. _____

  8. _____

  9. _____

 10. _____

 11. _____

 12. _____

 13. _____

Draw a map of the colony and label it with its name.

Ben Franklin Sails over the Ocean, Part I

Benjamin Franklin arrived in London on Christmas Eve of 1724. Planning to set up his own presses in Philadelphia, Ben went to England to buy printing equipment and establish business connections. Voyages across the Atlantic Ocean at that time generally took about three weeks, and conditions on many of the ships were very harsh. However, Ben lived "uncommonly well" in the great cabin, according to his journal. On his trip, he took letters of introduction from Pennsylvania's Governor Keith.

Your Assignment:

You are sailing to London with Benjamin Franklin. Ben says to you, "Pack any items that you want. Space is not a problem. What you take can be from today's world or from the past." Make a list of your goods.

(Example: radio)

_____   _____

_____   _____

_____   _____

_____   _____

_____   _____

_____   _____

_____   _____

_____   _____

_____   _____

From *13 Colonies! 13 Years! Integrating Content Standards and the Arts to Teach the American Revolution.* By Mary Wheeler and Jill Terlep. Music by Mary Wheeler. Illustrations by Jill Terlep. Westport, CT: Libraries Unlimited/Teacher Ideas Press. Copyright © 2006.

NAME _____ DATE _____

Ben Franklin Sails over the Ocean, Part II

Read your list to a partner. Listen as your partner reads his or her list to you. Then answer the following questions about <u>your partner's</u> packed items. (You cannot look at your partner's list again or ask any more questions.)

In your partner's list, what item is the …

1.   biggest?

_____

2.   smallest?

_____

3.   most unusual?

_____

4.   funniest?

_____

5.   best one that you didn't think of?

_____

6.   one that Ben Franklin might also have taken?

_____

7.   most practical item that your partner chose?

_____

8.   thing that your family would have enjoyed the most?

_____

9.   one your partner took that you would not have packed?

_____

10.   Whose list would keep your shipmates entertained? Why?

_____

COMPARISON TABLE OF 13 STATES, 1770 AND 2000
Populations and Capitals

State	Population/1770 (Estimated)	Population/2000 (Census)	Capital/1770	Capital/2000
Connecticut	183,900	3,405,565	New Haven/ Hartford	Hartford
Delaware	35,500	783,600	New Castle/ Dover	Dover
Georgia	23,400	8,186,453	Savannah	Atlanta
Maryland	202,600	5,296,486	Annapolis	Annapolis
Massachusetts	235,300	6,349,097	Boston	Boston
New Hampshire	62,400	1,235,786	Portsmouth	Concord
New Jersey	117,400	8,414,350	Perth Amboy	Trenton
New York	162,900	18,976,457	New York	Albany
North Carolina	197,200	8,049,313	New Bern	Raleigh
Pennsylvania	240,100	12,281,054	Philadelphia	Harrisburg
Rhode Island	58,200	1,048,319	Newport	Providence
South Carolina	124,200	4,012,012	Charles Town	Columbia
Virginia	447,000	7,078,515	Richmond	Richmond

From *13 Colonies! 13 Years! Integrating Content Standards and the Arts to Teach the American Revolution.* By Mary Wheeler and Jill Terlep. Music by Mary Wheeler. Illustrations by Jill Terlep. Westport, CT: Libraries Unlimited/Teacher Ideas Press. Copyright © 2006.

NAME _____ DATE _____

Changing Table, Part I

Use the *Comparison Table of 13 States, 1770 and 2000* to complete the answers.

Which state had the …

1. largest population in 1770?   _____

2. largest population in 2000?   _____

3. smallest population in 1770?   _____

4. smallest population in 2000?   _____

5. population of 1,235,786 in 2000?   _____

Compare the populations, and choose the correct symbol (< or >).

In 1770

6. Connecticut   _____   Georgia

7. North Carolina _____   New Jersey

8. Massachusetts _____   Pennsylvania

9. Delaware   _____   Rhode Island

10. New York   _____   South Carolina

In 2000

11. Maryland   _____   Virginia

12. North Carolina _____   Georgia

13. New Hampshire _____   Rhode Island

14. Connecticut   _____   South Carolina

15. Massachusetts _____   Delaware

From *13 Colonies! 13 Years! Integrating Content Standards and the Arts to Teach the American Revolution.* By Mary Wheeler and Jill Terlep. Music by Mary Wheeler. Illustrations by Jill Terlep. Westport, CT: Libraries Unlimited/Teacher Ideas Press. Copyright © 2006.

What is the difference between the populations of …

16. Georgia in 1770 and in 2000? _____

17. New Hampshire and Rhode Island in 2000? _____

18. South Carolina in 1770 and in 2000? _____

19. Virginia and Massachusetts in 1770? _____

20. Delaware and New Jersey in 1770? _____

Name the capital of …

21. Connecticut when the population was 3,405,565.

_____

22. the state whose population was 162,900 in 1770.

_____

23. Pennsylvania in 1770.

_____

24. New York in 2000.

_____

25. the state whose population was approximately 12 million in 2000.

_____

Calculate the average population of the 13 colonies in 1770.

_____

From *13 Colonies! 13 Years! Integrating Content Standards and the Arts to Teach the American Revolution.* By Mary Wheeler and Jill Terlep. Music by Mary Wheeler. Illustrations by Jill Terlep. Westport, CT: Libraries Unlimited/Teacher Ideas Press. Copyright © 2006.

NAME _____ DATE _____

Changing Table, Part II

Make a bar graph of the populations of the 13 states in 1770 or 2000. Be sure to label each axis, horizontal and vertical.

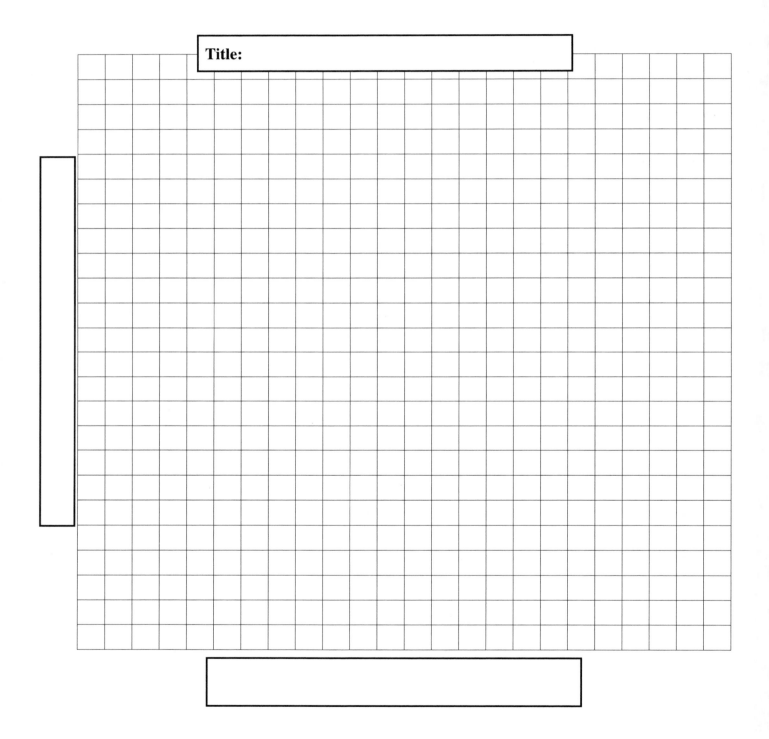

Title:

Rally around Your Flag

Suppose you could have designed the flag for our country during the American Revolution. What would it have looked like? Draw it. Then write a national motto.

(Motto)

From *13 Colonies! 13 Years! Integrating Content Standards and the Arts to Teach the American Revolution.* By Mary Wheeler and Jill Terlep. Music by Mary Wheeler. Illustrations by Jill Terlep. Westport, CT: Libraries Unlimited/Teacher Ideas Press. Copyright © 2006.

NAME _____ DATE _____

We the (Other) People

Have you ever heard of Deborah Sampson or Oconostota? Write a research report about Native Americans (Oneida, Cherokee, Iroquois, or another nation) or indentured servants. Prepare a two-minute presentation to your group; include at least two audiovisual aids, such as a map, drawing, list, graph, photo, song, or PowerPoint presentation.

Oh, yes! Someone in your group will identify Deborah Sampson and Oconostota. Maybe it'll be you!

Topic:

_____

Notes:

_____

_____

_____

_____

_____

_____

_____

_____

_____

_____

_____

_____

_____

_____

_____

_____

Native American wearing a Gustoweh
Just for fun ... Look it up.

From *13 Colonies! 13 Years! Integrating Content Standards and the Arts to Teach the American Revolution.* By Mary Wheeler and Jill Terlep. Music by Mary Wheeler. Illustrations by Jill Terlep. Westport, CT: Libraries Unlimited/Teacher Ideas Press. Copyright © 2006.

Electrical Problems

Solve the problems. Match the answers in the riddle. Write the letters in the blanks below to solve the riddle.

O

1. 125
    x   135

E

2. 25)‾4150‾

H

3. 5898
    23456
    155
    +   89

W

4. 96653
    − 25852

S

5. 558
    x   13

N

6. 33)‾1485‾

K

7. 6887
    − 1758

T

8. 189
    5898
    469
    + 4888

G

9. 156
    x 78

C

10. 11110
     − 1199

I

11. 39)‾8775‾

A

12. 789
     2500
     134
     +   19

D

13. 8478
     − 5665

What did Ben Franklin say when he discovered that lightning was electricity?

___   ___   ___   ___   ___   ___   _____ .
45   16,875   11,444   29, 598   225   45   12,168

___   ___   ___   ___   ___   ___   ___   ___
29,598   166   70,801   3,442   7,254   11,444   16,875   16,875

___   ___   ___   ___   ___   ___   ___ .
7,254   29,598   16,875   9,911   5,129   166   2,813

From *13 Colonies! 13 Years! Integrating Content Standards and the Arts to Teach the American Revolution.* By Mary Wheeler and Jill Terlep. Music by Mary Wheeler. Illustrations by Jill Terlep. Westport, CT: Libraries Unlimited/Teacher Ideas Press. Copyright © 2006.

Runaway Hornbook

Here's the middle of a story about an ordinary school day in a town in Massachusetts in the year of 1775. What happened in the beginning and ending? Finish the story.

Title _____

_____

_____

_____

_____

_____

All of a sudden, Penelope grabbed her hornbook and ran out the back door of the schoolhouse!

_____

_____

_____

_____

_____

_____

_____

_____

From *13 Colonies! 13 Years! Integrating Content Standards and the Arts to Teach the American Revolution.* By Mary Wheeler and Jill Terlep. Music by Mary Wheeler. Illustrations by Jill Terlep. Westport, CT: Libraries Unlimited/Teacher Ideas Press. Copyright © 2006.

It's a Match!

The 13 Colonies Map

New Hampshire

E*

New York

P*

Massachusetts

N*

H

M* F*

Rhode Island

Pennsylvania

Connecticut

O*

I*

New Jersey

L*

S

R*

K*

Delaware

Virginia

Maryland

G*

A*

C*

North Carolina

J*

Q*

South Carolina

D*

Georgia

B*

The Colonies, 1770

From *13 Colonies! 13 Years! Integrating Content Standards and the Arts to Teach the American Revolution.* By Mary Wheeler and Jill Terlep. Music by Mary Wheeler. Illustrations by Jill Terlep. Westport, CT: Libraries Unlimited/Teacher Ideas Press. Copyright © 2006.

NAME _____ DATE _____

It's a Match

Locate the following historical sites of the American Revolution on the 13 colonies map. Write the matching letter next to the place.

Battles:

_____   1.   Bunker Hill (Breed's Hill), Massachusetts (1775)

_____   2.   Saratoga, New York (1777)

_____   3.   Yorktown, Virginia (1781)

_____   4.   Cowpens, South Carolina (1781)

_____   5.   Monmouth, New Jersey (1778)

_____   6.   Long Island, New York (1776)

_____   7.   Charleston, South Carolina (1780)

Capitals in 1770:

_____   8.   Savannah, Georgia

_____   9.   Annapolis, Maryland

_____   10.   New Haven, Connecticut

_____   11.   New Bern, North Carolina

_____   12.   Portsmouth, New Hampshire

_____   13.   Richmond, Virginia

_____   14.   Newport, Rhode Island

From *13 Colonies! 13 Years! Integrating Content Standards and the Arts to Teach the American Revolution.* By Mary Wheeler and Jill Terlep. Music by Mary Wheeler. Illustrations by Jill Terlep. Westport, CT: Libraries Unlimited/Teacher Ideas Press. Copyright © 2006.

Events:

_____	15. Boston Tea Party; Boston, Massachusetts
_____	16. Constitutional Convention; Philadelphia, Pennsylvania
_____	17. Home of George Washington; Mt. Vernon, Virginia
_____	18. George Washington Wintered Troops in 1777–1778; Valley Forge, Pennsylvania
_____	19. Women Organized Tea Boycott; Edenton, Pennsylvania

20. Label the Appalachian Mountains on the map.

Extra Credit:

Make a scene. Choose a battle, city capital, or event and draw a picture of it.

From *13 Colonies! 13 Years! Integrating Content Standards and the Arts to Teach the American Revolution.* By Mary Wheeler and Jill Terlep. Music by Mary Wheeler. Illustrations by Jill Terlep. Westport, CT: Libraries Unlimited/Teacher Ideas Press. Copyright © 2006.

Gifted and Talented

Consider *13 Colonies! 13 Years!* to be a vehicle transporting student development beyond the traditional classroom. The Teacher Resource section of the book guides the pupils through the history of the American Revolution, and the play carries their imaginations and thoughts to new levels. Children truly become excited about the educational trip.

Doors open to new avenues for learning. So follow the path of students' interests, and treasure the journeys.

Are they actors, artists, comedians, teachers, inventors, leaders, debaters, photographers, speakers, musicians, or humanitarians?

Does the idea of writing, composing, designing, cooking, or sewing excite them?

What about construction, architecture, woodworking, farming, and education?

Do they want to learn more about the theatre, ecology, genealogy, or botany?

Physical activities—are they dancers, competitive athletes, or game players and strategists?

Are they fascinated by history, philosophy, poetry, geography, religion, science, or mathematics?

When children discover colonial American areas of study that excite their curiosity, their learning spirals upward. Encourage them to pursue those interests. For ideas beyond the worksheets, be sure to check the *Cross Curriculum ... More!* section of the book. It's full of great activities.

During the production of the play, taking advantage of the students' special gifts, inclinations, and talents works out well. If possible, allow some of them to assume responsibilities, either limited or complete, as managers, helpers, and leaders. Think about using children in any of the following jobs:

Student Director—works with the instructor, leads practices, and helps in overall management of production

Props Manager—makes sure props are ready, organizes their storage, and ensures that the production runs smoothly

Music Maestro—conducts the singers and choir in one or more songs, practices with small groups of performers, and provides input for musical performances

Costume Designer—makes outfits as suggested in the book or fashions patterns and sews better ones

Choreographer—creates hand motions for choir members and dance steps for songs like *Powder Your Wigs* and teaches them to participants

Instrumental Musician—plays drums and rhythms and accompanies songs on the piano, fifes, flutes, or other instruments

Set Constructor—builds suggested sets from the book or adds more innovative plans for scenery

Photographer—records activities, practices, and performances for graphic records

Videographer—films practices and performances

Decorator—takes charge of hanging or arranging the displays for the show

Drama Coach—works with small groups or individuals to improve deliveries and memorize lines

Journalist—maintains a written record of the proceedings

Set Artist—creates props and decorations

Sound Manager—runs the amplifiers and sound systems

Lighting Assistant—positions and maintains the spotlights and other lighting effects

The performance of the play is not the end, but the beginning. Remind your students to continue to thank the delegates to the Constitutional Convention and our forefathers for providing the framework for our great country. Using our ancestors as inspiration, challenge the children to use their skills and abilities to make a difference.

Cross Curriculum ...
More Activities!

All of the following activities are social studies related, and additional curriculum areas are noted.

Music

Learn about favorite tunes sung during the Revolution, such as "Soldier, Soldier, Will You Marry Me?"; "Michael Row the Boat Ashore"; or "We Gather Together." Organize a sing-a-long.

Plan a dance. Learn how to do the Virginia Reel, the minuet, and other 18th-century dances.

Art

Make a paper quilt. Using a ruler and pencil, design a pattern on a square piece of paper. Add colors. Have a "quilting bee," and tape all of the squares together in a quilt shape. Display the finished product. (A real one could even be made from cloth squares.)

Build a dry goods store typical of the era. Learn about products necessary and available to 18th-century Americans. Construct the building with large cardboard boxes, like refrigerator boxes, with the students drawing, coloring, and painting the furniture and items for sale.

Make a collage. Include pictures, maps, or other graphic sources in magazines about the Revolutionary times. Add drawings.

Draw or paint a mural depicting 18th-century life or events of the Revolution.

Have a "Funnies" contest.

- Make a cartoon about a late-18th-century subject.
- Don't put names on the works.
- Later, number the completed cartoons.
- Scramble the drawings and place them on different students' desks.
- "Snake" around the room reading the comic on each desk.
- When the teacher rings a bell or gives a signal, change to the next seat. (Giggle, but don't talk.) It's a quiet activity.
- Note the numbers of three favorite cartoons.
- When everyone has enjoyed all of the drawings, vote on the class's choice as the best.
- Congratulate, give prizes, and display the top three winners' entries.

Science and Technology

Plan menus, research recipes, and cook dishes of the era, such as Virginia ham, carrot puffs, or onion soup. What kinds of herbs were used? What about eating cooked rabbits or poultry served with their heads and feet attached as they did in Revolutionary days? Have a discussion. Enjoy an 18th-century meal (without the heads and feet, maybe?).

Research medicine and methods of treatment used by Native Americans or colonists.

Learn about the people who performed surgeries and dispensed remedies.

What were common diseases of the era?

Research which crops were grown in the colonies, for both personal and commercial purposes.

Study colonial habits of sanitation and their effects on quality of life.

Invent something. How did Ben Franklin's inventions change people's lifestyles?

Physical Education

Find out about popular games of the period such as marbles, ninepins, or rolling a hoop. Try playing some of them, and make up new ones appropriate for the time.

Math

Make timelines for revolutionary battles, speeches, and related events.

Using a road map, plan an imaginary (or real) car trip to battlefields, homes of famous figures, or historical sites. Figure distances, and use scales to determine mileage.

Make a flowchart for the events and documents list or related subjects.

Create an American Revolutionary PowerPoint presentation for the class. It could be an original poem with illustrations, biographical information, a historical event, or a Native American activity.

Following directions, make candles like they used to do in Colonial times.

Language Arts

Invite outside speakers to address the class. People to ask might be historical society members, state tourism officials, museum curators, local authors, government officials, skilled artisans, and community experts. Guests can address the class, and then conduct question-and-answer discussions.

Or conduct press conferences with the speakers. Set up the classroom like a mini-news station. Question the people and record their responses. Follow up the events by writing articles about the invited visitors and topics. Prior to the appearances, discuss respectful behavior toward visitors. Letter-writing activities precede and follow the events, too. Beforehand, write invitations to speakers from the class. Afterward, compose thank you letters.

Copy the song lyrics or poetry from overhead transparencies. Practice cursive writing, memorize the words, and learn history while writing the poetry. This is a good once or twice a week activity.

Have a debate. Draw names from a hat or choose sides to defend whether the colonies should declare independence or remain loyal British subjects. Research significant colonial Americans' opinions on independence. Encourage students to quote and credit noted historical speakers in the debate.

Make a list of books and related materials about the American Revolution that are available in the school or local library. Vote on a passage or book to read together as a group. Post your suggested reading list outside your classroom or in your library, if allowed, for others to enjoy.

Write speeches. Become *orators* and speak to the members of the Constitutional Convention (the class). Thank them for their efforts. Be specific with reasons.

Study independently at learning stations. Packets can contain music/rhymes, background information, vocabulary, and worksheets.

Make a class booklet. Include the Revolutionary stories and drawings. Share it with another class or with visitors to the room. Display it in the media center or library.

Report on a day in the life of a Native American or woman of the era.

Write a Revolutionary story. It might be about a

- soldier captured by the British.
- Native American who was hunting for food.
- family whose relative was fighting the war.
- person trying to convince other colonists of the need for our country's independence.
- British soldier relating his experience about being away from home.
- woman organizing a tea boycott.

Bring in related artifacts from the era. Have "Show and Tell."

Design a newspaper advertisement or write a radio/television commercial for a popular product used and sold during the Revolution. Show and explain the ad, or deliver the commercial to the class.

Rate a job. Study the Occupations section in the book. On a scale of 1 to 10, record personal interest in the occupations. Discuss reasons for decisions and numbers.

Find out how hornbooks were used by children in colonial schools and then make one. Select a student "teacher" to instruct the class with its hornbooks.

Locate a copy of *George Washington's Rules for Civility*. Read the maxims to a partner. Between the two of you, select the 10 most important rules. Share those statements and reasons for choosing them with the group.

Compose make-believe journal entries written by fictional characters of the colonial period.

Address specific historical questions like the following:

- What were the costs and expenses of conducting a Revolution in 1776?

- What was the U.S. relationship with foreign countries like France or Spain during the Revolution?

- How did Native Americans' roles and perspectives differ with those of the Patriots during the war?

- Did the Treaty of Paris contain terms of concessions only for the British?

- Where did immigrants settle, and why did they come to America?

Answer Key

Revolutionary Era Overview, page 13

1. B	6. B	11. C	16. A
2. C	7. A	12. C	17. B
3. A	8. C	13. A	18. A
4. C	9. C	14. B	19. B
5. C	10. C	15. C	20. C

13 Colonies! 13 Years!, page 16
(any order)

1. Massachusetts	5. North Carolina	9. New Jersey	13. Georgia
2. Pennsylvania	6. South Carolina	10. Maryland	
3. Connecticut	7. New Hampshire	11. Virginia	
4. Delaware	8. New York	12. Rhode Island	

Frankly, Mr. Franklin, page 19

1. False	6. True	11. False	16. False
2. False	7. True	12. True	17. False
3. True	8. False	13. False	18. False
4. False	9. False	14. True	19. True
5. True	10. False	15. True	20. True

Wisdom of the Ages, page 20

1. Well done is better than well said.
2. Observe all men; thyself most.
3. No gains without pains.
4. The Things which hurt, instruct.
5. He that won't be counsell'd, can't be help'd.
6. You may delay, but Time will not.
7. He that cannot obey, cannot command.
8. Haste makes Waste.
9. 'Tis easier to prevent bad habits than to break them.

The Ballad of John Paul Jones, page 24

1. Scotland
2. gardener
3. Captain
4. France
5. *Bonhomme Richard*
6. "I have not yet begun to fight."
7. *Serapis*
8. It sank.
9. Benjamin Franklin
10. Annapolis, Maryland
11. John Paul
12. He wanted to be free.

Independence Battle Rap, page 28
(any order)

Lexington	Concord	Princeton	Trenton
Lake Champlain (Fort Ticonderoga)	Bunker Hill	Saratoga	Valley Forge
Long Island	Harlem Heights	Monmouth	Savannah
Fort Washington	New York City	Charleston	Cowpens
Yorktown			

Constitutional Convention, page 36

1. Philadelphia
2. 1787
3. George Washington
4. Grand Convention
5. Benjamin Franklin
6. Alexander Hamilton
7. James Madison
8. James Madison
9. Paterson of New Jersey
10. Connecticut Compromise

Colonial Terms Crossword Puzzle, answers found on *Answer Key, Crossword Puzzles*

Separate, but Equal, page 42
(any order)

Congress	President	Supreme Court
Makes the laws	Carries out the laws	Decides whether laws are constitutional
Approves treaties	Conducts relations with other countries	Explains the meaning of treaties
Approves appointments	Is commander-in-chief	Decides legal cases
Can declare war	Manages the government	Decides cases between states

From *13 Colonies! 13 Years! Integrating Content Standards and the Arts to Teach the American Revolution.* By Mary Wheeler and Jill Terlep. Music by Mary Wheeler. Illustrations by Jill Terlep. Westport, CT: Libraries Unlimited/Teacher Ideas Press. Copyright © 2006.

What Does It Mean?, page 43

1. independence
2. ancestor
3. militia
4. tax
5. declaration
6. inauguration
7. cannon
8. boycott
9. checks and balances
10. *Poor Richard's Almanack*
11. D
12. G
13. C
14. H
15. B
16. E
17. I
18. A
19. J
20. F

Revolutionary Figures Crossword Puzzle, answers found on *Answer Key, Crossword Puzzles*

Revolutionary Figures Math Assessment, page 48

1. J (1744–1818)
2. B (1735–1826)
3. L (1738–1789)
4. I (1723–1770)
5. K (1728–1805)
6. A (1706–1790)
7. M (1755–1804)
8. P (1736–1799)
9. O (1743–1826)
10. D (1747–1792)
11. C (1760–1820)
12. E (1751–1836)
13. N (1737–1809)
14. G (1747–1825)
15. F (1723–1799)
16. H (1753–1784)
Bonus: about 67 years

George Washington Was the Best President, page 49

1. opinion
2. fact
3. fact
4. fact
5. opinion
6. fact
7. opinion
8. fact
9. opinion
10. fact
11. opinion
12. fact
13. fact

Occupations of the Era Crossword Puzzle, answers found on *Answer Key, Crossword Puzzles*

I Need Help. Whom Shall I Call?, page 54

1. blacksmith
2. cooper
3. tailor
4. miller
5. wainwright
6. blockprinter
7. hornsmith
8. bell founder
9. barber
10. chandler

(Three important artisans, any answers acceptable)

11. B
12. L
13. D
14. H
15. F
16. J
17. G
18. I
19. A
20. C

Events and Documents Crossword Puzzle, answers found on *Answer Key, Crossword Puzzles*

"Why Stand We Here Idle?" Let's Act Up!, page 59

1. Saratoga Battle, 1777
2. First Continental Congress, 1774
3. Intolerable Acts, 1774
4. Battle of Bunker Hill, 1775
5. *Common Sense*, Jan. 1776
6. Second Continental Congress, 1775
7. Connecticut Compromise, 1787
8. Constitution of the United States, 1787
9. Shay's Rebellion, 1787
10. Articles of Confederation, 1781
11. F
12. A
13. G
14. C
15. K
16. S
17. L
18. P
19. B
20. H

Whence You Came, Part I, page 67

1. Thomas Paine, *Common Sense*
2. Preamble to the Constitution of the United States
3. Declaration of Independence
4. Patrick Henry, Virginia House of Burgesses Speech
5. George Washington, Inaugural Address, April 30, 1789
6. Abigail Adams, Letter to John Adams, March 31, 1776

Changing Table, Part I, page 78

1. Virginia
2. New York
3. Georgia
4. Delaware
5. New Hampshire
6. >
7. >
8. <
9. <
10. >
11. <
12. <
13. >
14. <
15. >

16. 8,163,053
17. 187,467
18. 3,887,812
19. 211,700
20. 81,900
21. Hartford
22. New York
23. Philadelphia
24. Albany
25. Harrisburg
26. 160,777 (rounded)

We the (Other) People, page 82

Oconostoca was a Cherokee Native American, and Deborah Sampson was an indentured servant.

Electrical Problems, page 83

1. 16,875
2. 166
3. 29,598
4. 70,801
5. 7,254
6. 45
7. 5,129
Nothing. He was too shocked.

8. 11,444
9. 12,168
10. 9,911
11. 225
12. 3,442
13. 2,813

It's a Match, page 86

1. N
2. E
3. A
4. Q
5. I
6. S
7. D
8. B
9. R
10. M

11. J
12. P
13. G
14. F
15. H
16. L
17. K
18. O
19. C
20. Western Border of Colonies (Appalachian Mts.)

From *13 Colonies! 13 Years! Integrating Content Standards and the Arts to Teach the American Revolution.* By Mary Wheeler and Jill Terlep. Music by Mary Wheeler. Illustrations by Jill Terlep. Westport, CT: Libraries Unlimited/Teacher Ideas Press. Copyright © 2006.

Answer Key – Crossword Puzzles

Colonial Terms Crossword Puzzle, page 44

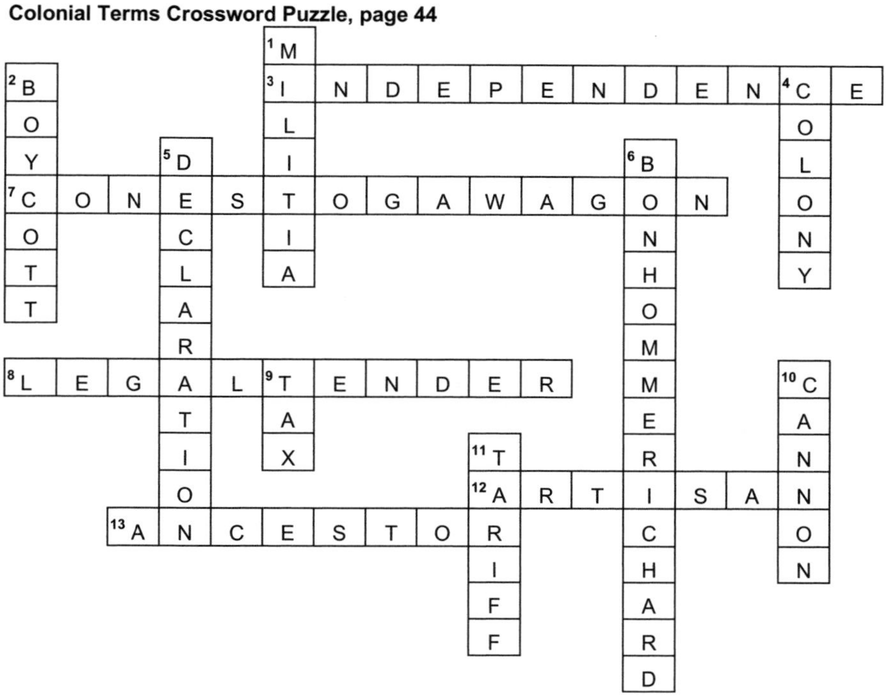
1 MILITIA
2 BOYCOTT
3 INDEPENDENCE
4 COLONY
5 DECLARATION
6 BONHOMMERICHARD
7 CONESTOGAWAGON
8 LEGALTENDER
9 TAX
10 CANNON
11 TARIFF
12 ARTISAN
13 ANCESTOR

Revolutionary Figures Crossword Puzzle, page 47

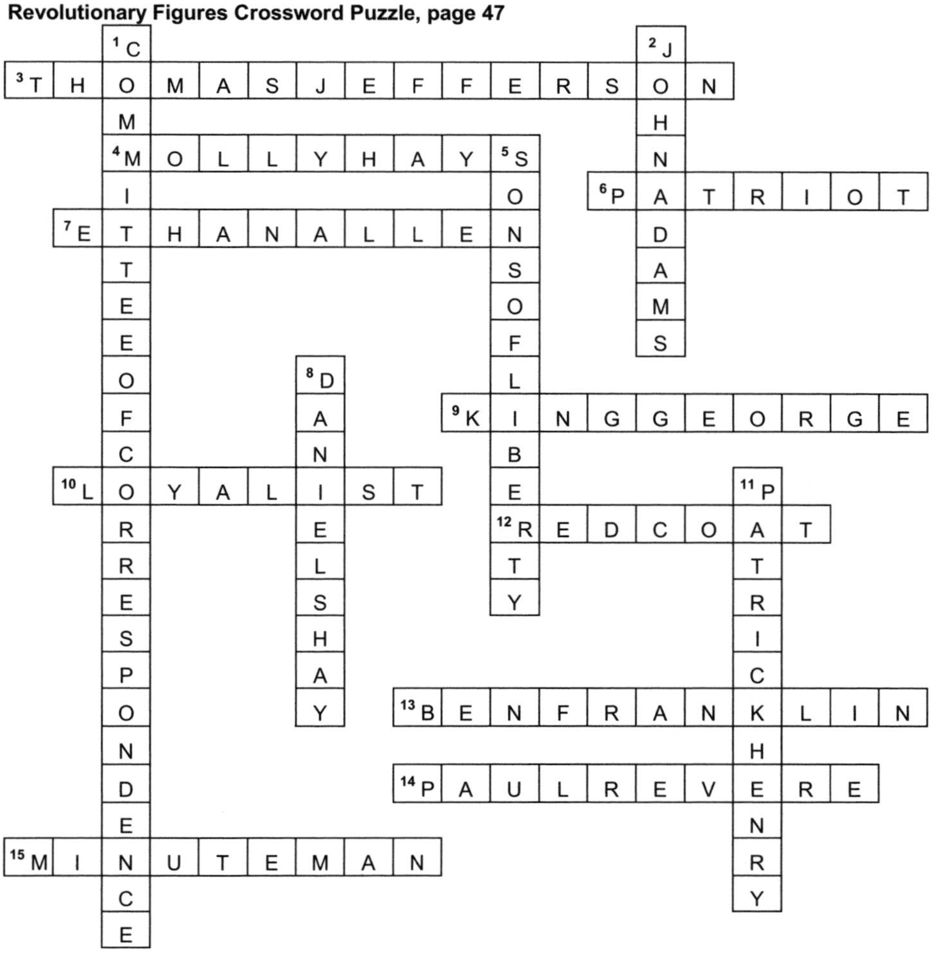
1 COMMITTEEOFCORRESPONDENCE
2 JOHNADAMS
3 THOMASJEFFERSON
4 MOLLYHAYS
5 SONSOFLIBERTY
6 PATRIOT
7 ETHANALLEN
8 DANIELSHAY
9 KINGGEORGE
10 LOYALIST
11 PATRICKHENRY
12 REDCOAT
13 BENFRANKLIN
14 PAULREVERE
15 MINUTEMAN

Occupations of the Era Crossword Puzzle, page 52

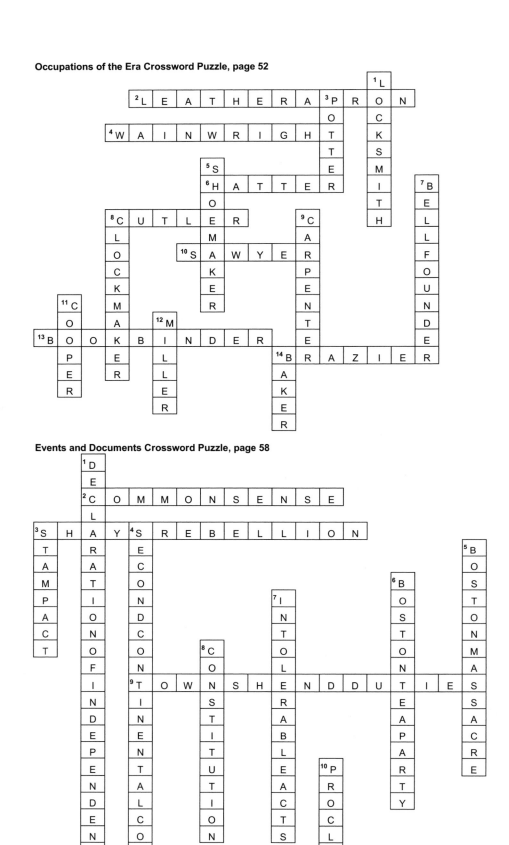

Events and Documents Crossword Puzzle, page 58

The Play

Play Synopsis

A stamp, glass, bell, and tea come to life! Curious about their ancestors, Elvin Stamp, Poppa Bottle, Dora Bell, and Tia Bagwell search for their roots, and in the process they learn about the American Revolution. Through old pictures belonging to Poppa, the memorable characters discover interesting facts about their forefathers and our country's early struggle for independence. Those years, 1776–1789, were important in our nation's history, and everyone helps Dora ring in the celebration for *13 Colonies! 13 Years!*

Scenes and Musical Sequence

ACT 1
Scene 1: INTRODUCTION
13 Colonies! 13 Years! (Elvin, Dora, Stage Characters, and Choir)

Scene 2: Thomas Paine—*Common Sense*

ACT 2
Scene 1: DECLARATION OF INDEPENDENCE
Frankly, Mr. Franklin (Poppa, Elvin, Dora, Tia, Franklin, Stage Characters, and Choir)

Scene 2: Patrick Henry—Virginia House of Burgesses speech, 1775

ACT 3
Scene 1: BATTLE OF MONMOUTH
The Ballad of John Paul Jones (Tia, Stage Characters, and Choir)
Independence Battle Rap (Molly, Soldier, Stage Characters, and Choir)

Scene 2: Phillis Wheatley—"On Virtue"
Wisdom Is Higher (Stage Characters and Choir)

ACT 4
Scene 1: BLACKSMITH SHOP
Powder Your Wigs (Blacksmith, Wives, Stage Characters, and Choir)

Scene 2: Abigail Adams—Letter to John Adams, Continental Congress, March 31, 1776
Constitutional Convention [Chorus]—(Choir)

ACT 5
Scene 1: CONSTITUTIONAL CONVENTION
Constitutional Convention (Madison, Morris, Washington, Stage Characters, and Choir)
Sing in a Circle (Stage Characters and Choir)

Scene 2: George Washington—Inaugural Address, April 30, 1789

ACT 6
FINALE:
13 Colonies! 13 Years! (Stage Characters from All Scenes and Choir)

Song Notes

Solos and Special Directions

Switch singers' solos to suit the group. Many of the songs can be sung by characters other than those noted. Add choreography—dance steps or hand movements—to the songs, especially those done by the choir. They make the musical more enjoyable to perform and watch. Spotlight the choir as they sing.

13 Colonies! 13 Years!

Dora rings bells. Elvin sings verses. Stage Characters and Choir sing choruses.

Frankly, Mr. Franklin

Dora, Poppa, Elvin, and Tia sing verses. Franklin **speaks** during quotations. Stage Characters and Choir sing choruses and the words, "Mr. Franklin."

The Ballad of John Paul Jones

Tia sings verses. Stage Characters and Choir sing choruses.

Independence Battle Rap

Drummer or keyboard percussion plays military cadence. Molly and Soldier sing verses. Rap (talk) a verse, sing a verse, then Stage Characters and Choir sing choruses. Snap fingers if not using a percussion instrument.

Wisdom Is Higher

Stage Characters and Choir sing.

Powder Your Wigs

Blacksmith and Wives sing introduction and take turns singing verses. Stage Characters and Choir sing choruses. Dancers perform the actions sung in the verses, such as *"slash the sword, tumble like his locks, go in circles, fold your middle, stir the pot, ride to town,"* etc. The verses on this song are optional, perform all of them or select the actions that suit your group.

Constitutional Convention

Choir sings chorus to introduce Act 5, Constitutional Convention.

Madison and Washington **speak** or **sing** their quotes. Morris **speaks** as the narrator of the verses. Stage Characters and Choir sing choruses.

Sing in a Circle

Stage Characters and Choir sing.

13 Colonies! 13 Years!

Stage Characters from **all** acts sing on stage with Choir.

Cast of Characters and Costume List

Costumes can be as simple or elaborate as you want to make them.

Elvin Stamp: Bell-bottom pants; sideburns; sunglasses; cape; scarves; holds big, cardboard stamp

Dora Bell: Large sweatshirt or sweater with bells hanging from it; big paper cutout Christmas bell on head; enters and leaves through cardboard door

Poppa Bottle: Bottle-shaped, cardboard cutout, covered with clear plastic wrap to give a shiny effect; gray shower cap on head as bottle top

Tia Bagwell: Tea-bag outfit

Benjamin Franklin, George Washington, Thomas Jefferson, John Adams, James Madison, Gouverneur Morris, Thomas Paine, and Patrick Henry: Dark shoes with gold cardboard buckles; long socks, pulled up over pants' legs to look like knee pants; long-sleeved shirts; vests and/or waist-jackets; cotton wigs, with George's pulled back into ponytail; wire-rimmed glasses for Ben

Phillis Wheatley, Cobbler's Wife (Mrs. Charlton), Miller's Wife (Mrs. Baldwin), and Molly Pitcher: Dark, plain, long dress; or long skirt and blouse, with apron

Abigail Adams: Long dress, may be fancy with ruffles

Blacksmith: Dark shoes with gold cardboard buckles; long socks, pulled up over pants' legs to look like knee pants; long-sleeved shirt; dull-colored, bibbed apron

Soldier and Drummer (if shown): Same as blacksmith, without apron

Dancers: *Boys*—same outfit as Franklin's; three-cornered hats (can be old felt cowboy hats, pinned back); *Girls*– same outfit as Abigail Adams; *Everyone*—dull-colored, bibbed apron (representing leather aprons)

Choir: Any acceptable clothing of the period

Stage Hands: Dark clothing, or black T-shirts with printed words on the front, "Stage Hand"

Props and Stage Setup

Props and backdrops can be as simple or elaborate as you want to make them.

      Door, made from a cardboard box (for Dora Bell's entries and exits)
      Pair of black shoes
      Horseshoe
      Rubber mallet
      Handbell
      Long wooden stick used as rammer for cannon
      Doorbell (offstage) rung at different times to announce Dora
      Any speeches that aren't memorized
      Kettle drum or sound tape for FINALE
      Tape recorder
      Sound effects recording
      American Flag

Backdrop

Make a backdrop from a large piece of cardboard. Backdrop should be a little taller than the children. Paint the outline white so it looks like a snapshot. The middle can be painted any light color. For each act, change the objects in the "picture." The items can be constructed of paper, cloth, cardboard, etc. Cut and attach them with tape or Velcro to the cardboard.

ACT 2: Liberty Bell   *ACT 3: Cannon*   *ACT 4: Working Table*
ACT 5: Desk   *ACT 6: American Flag*

Stage Setup

The stage is divided into 3 sections:

- <u>Stage Right,</u> Dora's door in Act 1

- <u>Center Stage</u> is Scene 1 (Pictures) in Acts 2–6.

- <u>Stage Left</u> holds microphone for Scene 2 in Acts 1–5.

Stage Diagram

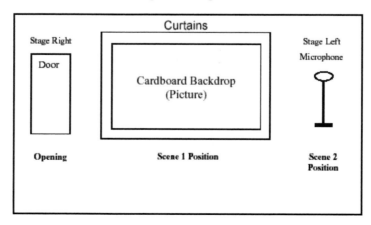

Prop Diagrams

Draw the bottle and stamp on heavy cardboard. Size is determined by the actors. Use paint, markers, fabric, and other materials to decorate. Punch holes and tie ribbons to hang the costume on the actors' necks.

Decorate the stamp with a picture of Elvis, a drawing of a guitar, or musical notes.

Cover bottle with clear plastic wrap to give a shiny effect. Use a gray shower cap on head as bottle top.

Elvin Stamp

USA 37

Poppa Bottle

Tia Bagwell (Tea Bag)

Draw the tea bag and tag on heavy cardboard.

Size is determined by the actors. Attach the tea bag tag to a knit cap. Use paint, markers, fabric, and other materials to decorate. Punch holes and tie ribbons to hang the costume on the actors' necks. Connect a wide ribbon or cardboard strip from bag to the hat.

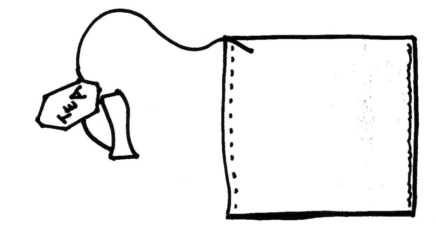

Play Performance Tips

Double Cast

Consider having two sets of the main characters: Elvin, Dora, Tia, and Poppa. This plan works well and gives more students an opportunity. Assign one group to Acts 1–3, and the second set to Acts 4–6. All the characters can appear in Act 6, the Finale.

Copies of the Script

To save time and money (both of which are often in short supply!), here are some tips on making copies of the play.

Adult volunteers can save a lot of time for you at the copy machine and are glad to help.

If your class is **reading the play aloud** and not performing for an audience, you will need enough copies of the entire play for each one or two students. Collect the stapled scripts at the end of the drama, and store them for next year.

For an **audience performance,** complete or partial scripts can be handed out.

- Main characters—Dora, Poppa, Elvin, and Tia—need all the pages. If you have two sets of main characters, give Acts 1–3 to the first group and Acts 4–6 to the second.

- Secondary characters—George Washington, Phillis Wheatley, Abigail Adams, Ben Franklin, Molly Pitcher, etc.—require only the sheets with their dialogs.

- Every performer, stage characters and the choir, should have copies of all of the song words.

All of the students will learn about the American Revolution by watching and performing.

If you intend to produce the play again next year, you may want to consider collecting all of the scripts at the end. Warn the children ahead of time if you expect them to return their copies when the play is over. (And plan on a few being lost or to be missing a few pages!)

Add or Eliminate Speakers

If additional students need to be involved, include more soldiers, wives, Constitutional Convention members, or artisans. Conversational lines can be added to the script to create more speaking parts. Announcers can welcome the audience and introduce the program, cast, and crew. Eliminate act(s) if not enough students are available. Actors can perform dual roles.

Presentation

Include dance steps or arm movements to go along with the choir music. Choreography makes the songs more enjoyable for the singers and more fun to watch.

When actors are not performing, they join the choir instead of remaining backstage. "Secret" traveling is done when the spotlight is on the opposite side of the stage. Children are responsible for their own moving times.

Stage a dress rehearsal for the whole school. Other classes can learn about the American Revolution, too!

Practice at least once with the spotlight(s) and microphones. Do a sound check and make sure all of the wires are plugged in.

Flexible Songs

Soloists are suggested, but change the singers to fit the individual class. Transpose the music for more suitable key ranges.

Make cue cards for the song *Powder Your Wigs* to give the dancers early notice of each new motion or verse. Cue cards should be invisible to the audience and have words like *go in circles, make a windmill, ride a horse,* etc.

Actors' Deliveries and Traveling

Caution students about "upstaging." When another cast member is speaking or singing, all others onstage should remain still. Encourage the actors to speak slowly and clearly and make eye contact often with the audience.

At the end of each act, the main characters should exit Stage Right. When Scene 2s are finished, the spotlight remains off as all main characters and "picture" characters take their places at center stage.

Videotape

Make sure the cameraperson sees a rehearsal to understand where the action will take place on stage. Sell the copies either as a fundraiser or to cover taping costs. Let the parents know ahead of time that they don't have to tape the entire program themselves. If you choose to sell videotapes, have all parents or guardians sign permission slips prior to the performance.

Stage Background *(if you want more than is required for the play)*

If your stage is bare and uninteresting, you may want to dress it up a bit. Hanging large letters, *13 Colonies! 13 Years!* can add balance and interest and brighten it up. Red, white, and blue streamers, available at most party stores, or other patriotic, decorative banners can be used for added cover.

Helpers

Enlist as many as possible—other teachers (especially art and music), upper grade students, parents, secretaries, administrators, language arts and social studies teachers, community members, etc. It is amazing how much help is available once the word is out. Parents do a terrific job of running spotlights, taking videotape orders, helping build backdrops, managing sound systems, and making costumes. High school students make wonderful choreographers.

Posters

Let the group decorate advertisements for the program. They can be made on poster board or construction paper. Distribute them throughout the school and community.

Programs

Include the children's names on the programs. They make great souvenirs. Students can submit drawings or computer-generated pictures for the program covers.

Publicity

Check with administrators to see if it's OK to alert local news sources about the presentation. Invite reporters to take pictures and write about the upcoming program. It's positive news about the school.

Timelines

Have the students make timelines about speeches, battles, or events that occurred during the Revolution. Plan a collective class timeline, one event per person. Display them during practices and on performance day for the audience.

Invitations

Write letters to the school board, parents, administrators, school staff, and other classes inviting them to attend. Practice good letter-writing techniques.

Reception and Wrap Party

A reception is a great way to celebrate postproduction enthusiasm. Following the performance, invite family members to join the cast and crew for coffee, punch, and snacks. A parents' group might be interested in organizing and hosting this event.

It's a wrap! During the next available day at school, rejoice together with a party. Watch the video, eat popcorn or treats, discuss the program, give pats on the backs, and have fun!

Off, Off, Off Broadway Singers

Encourage the group to have fun with the music. It's great if the students are always on pitch, but it rarely happens with the normal school group. So tell them to sing out and sing as best they can. The results are often off-key, but the experience is positively unforgettable (and will definitely make you smile!). With families and friends, you have a great biased audience that won't notice the "klinkers."

Homeschool Suggestions for the Play

Include the arts in the children's educational curriculum. Using this unique approach to teaching the history of the American Revolution stimulates students' academic and developmental growth. Because the play *13 Colonies! 13 Years!* uses simple props and backdrops, it can easily be adapted to most homeschool programs.

Adjust the material for small groups. Stage just one or two acts. Read the play aloud, and include any willing family members or neighbors as participants. Even the family pet can be written into the script. (How about the blacksmith's dog?)

Work with other families. Split the responsibilities for backdrops and props among other homeschool groups. Give Act 1 to one family, Act 2 to another, or divide the play to suit the group's size.

Separate children by age. What fits the situation? Older students can perform the main characters' roles. Dancers in *Powder Your Wigs* can be younger children.

Invite neighbors, church members, family, and friends to view the finished production. It's a great way for the children to share their talents and knowledge.

Create an auditorium. With simple backdrops, the play can be performed in a backyard, using the side of a house or a deck as the backstage. Sweep out the garage and use sheets to cover the lawn tools. Seat the audience in lawn chairs or on old blankets on the floor like a picnic. Ask the church, civic center, or public library for use of their meeting room. Many will let groups use the space for free. Use a home living room or den. Changing the area into a theater will be part of the fun.

Look for field trip opportunities. Search out museums, collections, and cultural attractions in the local area that feature American Revolutionary figures, lifestyles, and experiences. Extend the learning adventure by planning the destination of the next vacation to include American Revolutionary sites.

Let the book be a springboard that allows the children's natural learning curiosity to leap in new directions.

13 COLONIES! 13 YEARS!

Act 1: INTRODUCTION

Scene 1

(**Spotlight on stage right:** *Poppa and Elvin are on stage. Doorbell chimes offstage. Enter Dora Bell through the cardboard door.*)

Elvin: It's Dora Bell.

Dora: Hi, Elvin. Hi, Poppa.

Poppa: Here comes Miss Bagwell, too.

(*Enter Tia Bagwell through the door.*)

Tia: (*Walks in*) That's Tia Bagwell, Sir. (*Shakes hands with everyone*)

Elvin: Hmmm. You're Tia Bagwell, you say. Interesting. (*Slowly*) Tia Bagwell.

Poppa: Well, hello there, Tia. I'm Poppa Bottle, and these are my friends, Elvin Stamp and Dora Bell. You know, Tia, Elvin and I were just talking about how happy we are. Life has been very good to us.

Dora: Yes, Poppa. We sure are lucky to be living in the United States of America.

Tia: That's right. Our country wasn't always independent, as it is today. But because of our ancestors—tea, glass, and stamps—we have freedom in our country.

Dora: And my ancestors were always there to ring in the news.

Poppa: True. Our forefathers helped lead to the American Revolution, and that was when the colonists demanded independence from Great Britain. The British wanted to "stamp" things. You don't mind if I say that; do you, Elvin?

Elvin: (*Elvis imitation: looks to left with head, then right . . . moves straight legs*) That's all right, Poppa.

Poppa: Thanks. Well, that stamping was really taxation without representation.

Tia: And they were even taxing tea, too!

Elvin: From my great, great granddaddy I heard about the Stamp Act of 1765. It made a lot of people in the colonies mad, and changes started to happen.

Tia: The colonists boycotted the British goods until the tax was stopped.

From *13 Colonies! 13 Years! Integrating Content Standards and the Arts to Teach the American Revolution.* By Mary Wheeler and Jill Terlep. Music by Mary Wheeler. Illustrations by Jill Terlep. Westport, CT: Libraries Unlimited/Teacher Ideas Press. Copyright © 2006.

Elvin: Boycotted?

Poppa: Boycotted means refused to buy things. And the colonists even began to make their own paint, paper, and my ancestors—glass.

Tia: But the British kept trying to tax our colonists.

Poppa: Right, Tia, but those 1767 taxes, the Townshend Duties, were also repealed.

Tia: I know what came next. It was that awful Tea Act of 1773. It was a clever way to get colonists to buy tea again. But it didn't work.

Elvin: So we had the Boston Tea Party.

Tia: Yes, and all of my ancestors went swimming. And not in a tea cup either.

Poppa: We owe a lot to our ancestors. Let's look back at those thirteen years, 1776 to 1789, to see what happened again. You know, I have some old pictures of those times. Let's take a look.

Tia: Yes, back to 13 Colonies! 13 Years!

Dora: I'll help ring you back.

(Sing *13 Colonies! 13 years!*)

13 Colonies! 13 Years!

Chimes—(Ring—Ring—Ring—Ring)
1776 to 1789
Chimes—(Ring—Ring—Ring—Ring)

13 colonies, 13 years! 13 colonies, 13 years!
They started with a declaration,
Ended with inauguration.
Let us have a celebration, NOW!
13 colonies, 13 years! 13 colonies, 13 years!

Massachusetts, Pennsylvania, Connecticut, and Delaware,
North Carolina, South Carolina, Georgia—they all were there.

New Hampshire, New York, and New Jersey –
Everywhere church bells were heard.
Maryland, Virginia, and tiny Rhode Island—
They all opposed King George the Third.
Chimes—(Ring—Ring—Ring—Ring)

1776 to 1789
Chimes—(Ring—Ring—Ring—Ring)
13 colonies, 13 years! 13 colonies, 13 years!
They started with a declaration,
Ended with inauguration.
Let us have a celebration, NOW!
13 colonies, 13 years! 13 colonies, 13 years!
13 Colonies, 13 Years!

*(**Spotlight off.** Characters exit stage right.)*

From *13 Colonies! 13 Years! Integrating Content Standards and the Arts to Teach the American Revolution.* By Mary Wheeler and Jill Terlep. Music by Mary Wheeler. Illustrations by Jill Terlep. Westport, CT: Libraries Unlimited/Teacher Ideas Press. Copyright © 2006.

13 Colonies! 13 Years!

Mary Wheeler

From *13 Colonies! 13 Years! Integrating Content Standards and the Arts to Teach the American Revolution.* By Mary Wheeler and Jill Terlep. Music by Mary Wheeler. Illustrations by Jill Terlep. Westport, CT: Libraries Unlimited/Teacher Ideas Press. Copyright © 2006.

Scene 2

*(**Spotlight on stage left—Thomas Paine:** Thomas Paine enters as **Introduction** closes.)*

Thomas Paine: The date is January 9, 1776, and my pamphlet, *Common Sense,* has just been published. My name is Thomas Paine. In *Common Sense* I said,

"The sun never shined on a cause of greater worth. 'Tis not the affair of a city, a county, a province, or a kingdom; but of a continent—of at least one-eighth part of the habitable globe. 'Tis not the concern of a day, a year, or an age; posterity are virtually involved in the contest, and will be more or less affected even to the end of time by the proceedings now. Now is the seedtime of continental union, faith, and honor."

*(**Spotlight off.** Thomas Paine exits. As Thomas Paine is speaking, Thomas Jefferson and John Adams should secretly take their places in front of their picture. Poppa, Elvin, Dora Bell, and Tia should move to center stage.)*

From *13 Colonies! 13 Years! Integrating Content Standards and the Arts to Teach the American Revolution.* By Mary Wheeler and Jill Terlep. Music by Mary Wheeler. Illustrations by Jill Terlep. Westport, CT: Libraries Unlimited/Teacher Ideas Press. Copyright © 2006.

Act 2: DECLARATION OF INDEPENDENCE

Scene 1

Picture
[Thomas Jefferson and John Adams with the Liberty Bell]
Thomas Jefferson and John Adams are "frozen."

*(**Spotlight on center stage:** Poppa, Elvin, Dora Bell, and Tia are staring at "picture" of Thomas Jefferson and John Adams.)*

Poppa: Look, here's the first picture, and it's Thomas Jefferson and John Adams.

Thomas Jefferson: *(Comes to life; speaks very boldly)* "We hold these truths to be self-evident, that all men are created equal, that they are endowed by their Creator with certain unalienable Rights, that among these are Life, Liberty and the pursuit of Happiness."

Tia: Excuse me, excuse me. Are you reading from the Declaration of Independence?

Thomas Jefferson: *(Looking startled)* Uhhh, why yes. My friend, John Adams, and I served on a committee to write a resolution declaring our independence from Great Britain.

Poppa: I'm Poppa Bottle, and these are my friends, Dora Bell, Elvin Stamp, and Tia T. Bagwell.

John Adams: And here comes another of our committee members, Benjamin Franklin. He's a very wise man, you know. *Poor Richard's Almanack,* written by Mr. Franklin, is widely read throughout the colonies.

(Enter Benjamin Franklin.)

Elvin: Hello, Mr. Franklin. You probably think that we're kind of strange looking, but we're here to learn about the American Revolution.

Benjamin Franklin: *(Very serious)* Greetings. "He that would live in peace and at ease, must not speak all he knows, nor judge all he sees."

Dora: Frankly, Mr. Franklin, we are here to learn, and we could use some good advice. Would you please share a few of your thoughts?

(Sing *Frankly, Mr. Franklin*)

Frankly, Mr. Franklin

Frankly, Mr. Franklin, we need some good advice.
Some almanack quotations from Poor Richard would be nice.
Help us put our minds at ease
With these people; tell us please.
Frankly, Mr. Franklin, we need some good advice.

Sam invited company, served cake and soda pop.
Because he never smiled at all his party was a flop.
Mr. Franklin:
"If you would have guests merry with cheer, be so yourself, or so at least appear."

Susie did her math each day; she wanted a good grade.
But since she did not check her work, a "C" is what she made.
Mr. Franklin:
"Well done is twice done."

Frankly, Mr. Franklin, we need some good advice.
Some almanack quotations from Poor Richard would be nice.
Help us put our minds at ease
With these people; tell us please.
Frankly, Mr. Franklin, we need some good advice.

Mary was a lazy girl, would not get out of bed.
"We can't depend on her at all," her worried mother said.
Mr. Franklin:
"Lost time is never found again."

"Alice was a follower. She seldom used her mind.
When others "jumped into a lake," she wasn't far behind.
Mr. Franklin:
"There are lazy minds as well as lazy bodies."

Frankly, Mr. Franklin, we need some good advice.
Some almanack quotations from Poor Richard would be nice.
Help us put our minds at ease
With these people; tell us please.
Frankly, Mr. Franklin, we need some good advice.

"I am smarter than you are," that bragger, Bart, would say.
He wasn't smart enough to know why people stayed away.
Mr. Franklin:
"People who are wrapped up in themselves make small packages."

Frankly, Mr. Franklin, we need some good advice.
Some almanack quotations from Poor Richard would be nice.
Help us put our minds at ease
With these people; tell us please.
Frankly, Mr. Franklin, we need some good advice.

From *13 Colonies! 13 Years! Integrating Content Standards and the Arts to Teach the American Revolution.* By Mary Wheeler and Jill Terlep. Music by Mary Wheeler. Illustrations by Jill Terlep. Westport, CT: Libraries Unlimited/Teacher Ideas Press. Copyright © 2006.

Frankly, Mr. Franklin

Mary Wheeler

Dora: Hmmm. "Well done is twice done. Lost time is never found again." Thanks, Mr. Franklin, that's a lot to think about.

Poppa: We appreciate that advice, Mr. Franklin. And now we want to learn more about our ancestors and our country's history.

John Adams: Well, you're right about tea, glass, and stamps, your forefathers, and their important roles in the American Revolution.

Thomas Jefferson: Our anger has grown over many years, but one big problem has been Great Britain's government trying to tax our colonies to raise money for its own reasons. That terrible Stamp Act of 1765, Elvin, made us mad! Parliament said we had to buy stamps from a tax collector and stick them on many different items, like newspapers, business papers, ministers' sermons, and more.

John Adams: So, we formed the Sons of Liberty and organized a boycott of English goods. And Parliament repealed the Stamp Act in 1766. But the next year, Great Britain tried again to tax— things like paper, lead, paint, and even tea.

Tia: *(Indignant)* Tea? Did you say *tea*?

John Adams: Yes, and after that tea was dumped in Boston Harbor, King George III and Parliament wanted to punish the colonies, so they took away our right to self-government with the Intolerable Acts. *(Getting excited)* Pardon me, everyone. I just get awfully excited when I start talking about all of this.

Elvin: Me, too! I guess you could say that I'm all shook up.

Poppa: Don't say shook up to me, Elvin. If I were all shook up, I'd bubble over and blow my top!

Thomas Jefferson: Thomas Paine wrote that King George III is a "royal brute."

Dora: King George was a scoundrel!

Benjamin Franklin: But remember: "He that scatters thorns, let him not go barefoot."

Tia: The time has come to break away from King George III and England.

Elvin: It's now or never.

Tia: Right, Elvin.

Poppa: And so we come to the Declaration of Independence from which you were reading. Correct, Mr. Jefferson?

Thomas Jefferson: Yes, and it is being read throughout the colonies.

Benjamin Franklin: We know that "We must all hang together or we will all hang separately."

Dora: *(Ringing offstage)* Listen, can you hear the bells, my ancestors, announcing our independence?

John Adams: Yes, and soon we will ring this one. *(Points to Liberty Bell)*

From *13 Colonies! 13 Years! Integrating Content Standards and the Arts to Teach the American Revolution.* By Mary Wheeler and Jill Terlep. Music by Mary Wheeler. Illustrations by Jill Terlep. Westport, CT: Libraries Unlimited/Teacher Ideas Press. Copyright © 2006.

Thomas Jefferson: *(Resumes reading the Declaration of Independence. Bells ring softly in background.)* "That to secure these rights Governments are instituted among Men, deriving their just powers from the consent of the governed, That whenever any Form of Government becomes destructive of these ends, it is the Right of the People to alter or to abolish it, and to institute a new Government."

*(**Spotlight off.** Characters exit stage right.)*

From *13 Colonies! 13 Years! Integrating Content Standards and the Arts to Teach the American Revolution.* By Mary Wheeler and Jill Terlep. Music by Mary Wheeler. Illustrations by Jill Terlep. Westport, CT: Libraries Unlimited/Teacher Ideas Press. Copyright © 2006.

Scene 2

*(**Spotlight on stage left—Patrick Henry:** Patrick Henry enters as Declaration of Independence closes. As Patrick Henry speaks, remove Liberty Bell, and add cannon to backdrop for Battle of Monmouth.)*

Patrick Henry: It is spring 1775, and I am speaking to the members of the Virginia House of Burgesses. My name is Patrick Henry.

"Gentlemen may cry peace, peace—but there is no peace. The war is actually begun! The next gale that sweeps from the north will bring to our ears the clash of resounding arms! Why stand we here idle? What is it the gentlemen wish? What would they have: Is life so dear, or peace so sweet, as to be purchased at the price of chains and slavery? Forbid it, almighty God! I know not what course others may take; but as for me, give me liberty, or give me death!"

*(**Spotlight off.** Patrick Henry exits. As Patrick Henry is speaking, Molly Pitcher and Soldier should secretly take their places in front of their picture. Main characters reenter.)*

From *13 Colonies! 13 Years! Integrating Content Standards and the Arts to Teach the American Revolution.* By Mary Wheeler and Jill Terlep. Music by Mary Wheeler. Illustrations by Jill Terlep. Westport, CT: Libraries Unlimited/Teacher Ideas Press. Copyright © 2006.

Act 3: BATTLE OF MONMOUTH

Scene 1

Picture
[Molly Pitcher and Soldier with Cannon]
Molly Pitcher and Soldier are "frozen."

***(Spotlight on center stage:** Poppa, Elvin, Dora Bell, and Tia are staring at "picture" of Molly Pitcher and Soldier.)*

Poppa: This second picture is one of Molly Hays and a Patriot soldier at the Battle of Monmouth in New Jersey. Most people today know Mrs. Hays as Molly Pitcher. It's June 28, 1778.

Molly: *(Coming alive, wiping her brow)* What a day! It's so hot! It began with my carrying pitchers of water for the artillerymen who are serving with my husband, John.

Soldier: The heat has been awful. Many of the troops are suffering from sunstroke since the temperature is nearly 100 degrees. Both sides have had a lot of casualties, but Molly, here, has worked right along with us on the battlefield.

Dora: What happened, Molly?

Molly: Well, my husband, John, was unable to continue his job. Our side needed help. So I grabbed the rammer staff that he was using, and I swabbed and loaded the cannon, like I had seen him do so often. I had to do it! *(Demonstrates with rammer)*

Soldier: She was great, and I'm told that she'll be issued a warrant as a non-commissioned officer by General Washington tomorrow morning.

Molly: You know, lots of women have helped the Patriots. They've worked in army camps, washing, cooking, nursing; and some have gone, like me, onto the battlefields bringing food and water.

Tia: This war has been hard for everyone. There have been so many battles.

Poppa: Yes, and one of the most famous naval battle heroes is John Paul Jones.

(Sing *The Ballad of John Paul Jones*)

The Ballad of John Paul Jones

John Paul Jones was a hero;
He battled shore to shore.
He named his ship *Bonhomme Richard*
And sailed it off to war.

John Paul Jones left Scotland 'cause he wanted to be free.
He settled in the colonies, but John Paul loved the sea.
Americans refused a tax and firmly took a stand.
In the Continental Navy, John accepted a command.

From *13 Colonies! 13 Years! Integrating Content Standards and the Arts to Teach the American Revolution.* By Mary Wheeler and Jill Terlep. Music by Mary Wheeler. Illustrations by Jill Terlep. Westport, CT: Libraries Unlimited/Teacher Ideas Press. Copyright © 2006.

John Paul Jones was a hero;
He battled shore to shore.
He named his ship *Bonhomme Richard*
And sailed it off to war.

John's crew began to fire upon the mighty British fleet.
Although his ship was damaged, John would not accept defeat.
Captain Jones stood up and called above the cannons' roar,
"I have not yet begun to fight," and so they fought some more.

John Paul Jones was a hero;
He battled shore to shore.
He named his ship *Bonhomme Richard*
And sailed it off to war.

Bonhomme Richard was sinking fast. John took his valiant crew
Aboard a beaten English ship that knew that it was through.
John lost his ship, but won the fight. When all the smoke had cleared,
The news of John Paul's victory reached home, and people cheered.

John Paul Jones was a hero;
He battled shore to shore.
He named his ship *Bonhomme Richard*
And sailed it off to war.

"I have not yet begun to fight. I have not yet begun to fight."
His words still echo in our ears.
"I have not yet begun to fight. I have not yet begun to fight."
We do remember after all these years.

"I have not yet begun to fight. I have not yet begun to fight."
His words still echo in our ears.
"I have not yet begun to fight. I have not yet begun to fight."
We do remember after all these years.

From *13 Colonies! 13 Years! Integrating Content Standards and the Arts to Teach the American Revolution.* By Mary Wheeler and Jill Terlep. Music by Mary Wheeler. Illustrations by Jill Terlep. Westport, CT: Libraries Unlimited/Teacher Ideas Press. Copyright © 2006.

The Ballad of John Paul Jones

Mary Wheeler

Elvin: I would have been proud to serve along with John Paul Jones.

Molly: There were a lot of battles. They started with the Northern Campaign and the battles near Boston and New York.

Soldier: After General Washington retreated across the Delaware River, the fighting moved to New Jersey. And in 1777, areas near Philadelphia and Saratoga were important sites.

Poppa: And then came the terrible winter at Valley Forge. The British troops were spending the winter in Philadelphia homes, but General Washington marched our soldiers about 20 miles outside of the city. He wanted to discourage the Redcoats from advancing further.

Soldier: But it was awful for our men. They had been fighting for many months, and they were ragged and hungry.

Molly: Yes, and it was December and there was snow and the temperature was freezing. It was a bad winter.

Soldier: Because of diseases and hunger and cold, a lot of soldiers sickened and died. Even the horses were dying because of lack of feed.

Molly: But General Washington led by example; and although many lost their lives, those who managed to live were somehow stronger. When spring came, they thought it was a miracle!

Soldier: A new army came forth in the summer of 1778. They believed that they could meet any Redcoat challenge.

Poppa: So, it was on to the South, where the final victory at Yorktown was won. With the help of the French forces, the American troops forced Cornwallis to surrender his entire army.

Elvin: Surrender, you said, surrender ...

Dora: Cornwallis surrendered, Elvin. Gosh, it was "common sense" to declare independence, but it was a long and hard war.

(Sing *Independence Battle Rap*)

Independence Battle Rap

Common sense, common sense,
The Independence War.
Common sense, the Yankee Doodles fought for freedom evermore.

Lexington then Concord, that's where the war began.
"Got my musket, I am ready!" called the Minuteman.

Green Mountain Boys went marching up north to Lake Champlain.
The Patriots stormed the fort at dawn in a surprise campaign.

Common sense, common sense,
The Independence War.
Common sense, the Yankee Doodles fought for freedom evermore.

Redcoats met the Patriots, who battled hard, but still
With ammunition running low, they lost at Bunker Hill.

The New York City battles for our troops did not go well.
The year was 1776, but still too soon to tell.

Common sense, common sense,
The Independence War.
Common sense, the Yankee Doodles fought for freedom evermore.

On Christmas night George took his men across the Delaware.
At Princeton and at Trenton, he attacked the British there.

The Saratoga victory was led by General Gates.
This turning point in '77 helped seal our nation's fate.

Common sense, common sense,
The Independence War.
Common sense, the Yankee Doodles fought for freedom evermore.

Disease and awful weather plagued the Patriots, but George
Continued in the winter to have hope at Valley Forge.

Onward to the south they charged, and 1781
Brought victory at Yorktown, and our country had begun!

Common sense, common sense,
The Independence War.
Common sense, the Yankee Doodles fought for freedom evermore.

Independence Battle Rap

Mary Wheeler

Sing w/piano & drums

gan. "Got my mus-ket, I am rea-dy," called the Min-ute-man. *Molly* Green Moun-tain boys went
still, with am-mu-nit-ion run-ning low, they lost at Bun-ker Hill. The New York Ci-ty
ware. At Prince-ton and at Tren-ton he at-tacked the Brit-ish there. The Sar-a-to-ga
George con-tin-ued in the win-ter to have hope at Val-ley Forge. On-ward to the

march-ing up north to Lake Cham-plain. Pat-riots stormed the fort at dawn in
bat-tles for our troops did not go well. The year was Sev-en-teen Sev-en-ty Six, but
vic-to-ry was led by Gen-eral Gates. This turn-ing point in Sev-en-ty Seven helped
South they charged, and Sev-en-teen Eight-y One, brought vic-to-ry at York-town, and our

a sur-prise cam-paign. *All:* Com-mon sense, com-mon sense, the in-de-pen-dence war.
still too soon to tell.
seal our na-tion's fate.
coun-try had be-gun.

Com-mon sense, the Yan-kee Doo-dles fought for free-dom ev-er-more.

Fine (after verse 4)

Poppa: The Continental Congress ratified the Treaty of Paris on January 14, 1784. In the treaty, Britain pledged to respect American independence.

Tia: And we're proud to be Yankee Doodles, aren't we?

*(**Spotlight off.** Ring bell offstage. Characters exit stage right.)*

Scene 2

*(**Spotlight on stage left—Phillis Wheatley:** Phillis Wheatley enters as **Battle of Monmouth** closes. As Phillis Wheatley speaks, remove cannon, and add blacksmith table with forge for Blacksmith Shop.)*

Phillis Wheatley: My given name is Phillis Wheatley, and I was brought to this country from Africa in the year 1761 and sold as a slave. Though I received no formal education, I have learned to read and write, and I have endeavored to learn the Latin tongue. Through my writing, I have been invited by General George Washington to Cambridge, Massachusetts.

On Virtue

O THOU bright jewel, in my aim I strive
To comprehend thee Thine own words declare
Wisdom is higher than a fool can reach.
I cease to wonder and no more attempt
Thine height to explore, or fathom thy profound
But o my soul, sink not into despair;
Virtue is near thee, and with gentle hand
Would now embrace thee, —hovers o'er thine head...

(Sing *Wisdom Is Higher*)

Wisdom Is Higher

Who sailed? Who sailed?
Who sailed the ship across the sea?
He could bind
The chains around her legs,
But he could not restrain her mind.

Who sailed? Who sailed?
Who sailed the ship across the sea?
Away she climbed
With pen . . . and books for steps,
And so she left his chains behind.

"Wisdom is higher than a fool can reach.
Wisdom is higher than a fool can reach."
Higher, higher, higher, higher –
"Wisdom is higher than a fool can reach."

*(**Spotlight off.** Phillis Wheatley exits. As Wheatley is speaking, the blacksmith, Mrs. Baldwin, and Mrs. Charlton should secretly take their places in front of the picture. Main characters reenter.)*

Wisdom is Higher
(A Tribute to Phillis Wheatley)

Mary Wheeler

From *13 Colonies! 13 Years! Integrating Content Standards and the Arts to Teach the American Revolution.* By Mary Wheeler and Jill Terlep. Music by Mary Wheeler. Illustrations by Jill Terlep. Westport, CT: Libraries Unlimited/Teacher Ideas Press. Copyright © 2006.

Act 4: BLACKSMITH SHOP

Scene 1

Picture

**[Blacksmith, Cobbler's Wife, and Miller's Wife
with Forge in Shop]**

Blacksmith, Mrs. Baldwin, and Mrs. Charlton are "frozen."

*(**Spotlight on center stage:** Poppa, Elvin, Dora Bell, and Tia are staring at "picture" of Blacksmith, Mrs. Baldwin, and Mrs. Charlton.)*

Poppa: It's the village blacksmith and the wives of the cobbler and miller.

(Clanging noise in the background; picture characters come alive. Blacksmith swings hammer. Women begin to move. Cobbler's wife holds shoes.)

Blacksmith: Mrs. Baldwin, the shoes for your horse will be ready soon. I have a little more pounding to do. *(Pounds; clank, clank offstage)*

Mrs. Baldwin: Thank you, Mr. Reed. Since my husband is serving in the army for this battle for independence, it seems that his flourmill business has fallen to me. Even getting our horses' shoes.

Mrs. Charlton (Cobbler's Wife): And me, too. Here are your repaired shoes, Mr. Reed. My husband left last week to fight for the cause, so here I am delivering the cobbled shoes.

Elvin: Did someone say shoes? Horseshoes? Cobbled shoes? Blue suede shoes?

Tia: No, Elvin. Even the shoemaker didn't make blue suede shoes back then. But there were many skillful artisans.

Dora: Sure. There were printers, clockmakers, silversmiths, and bell founders, too, although most of the bronze is going for cannons now.

Blacksmith: Oh, yes. We have lots of good workers. We call ourselves *leather aprons* because we wear them to do our jobs.

(Dancers enter, perform the actions sung in the verses, like "slash the sword, tumble like his locks, go in circles, fold your middle, stir the pot, ride to town, etc.)

From *13 Colonies! 13 Years! Integrating Content Standards and the Arts to Teach the American Revolution.* By Mary Wheeler and Jill Terlep. Music by Mary Wheeler. Illustrations by Jill Terlep. Westport, CT: Libraries Unlimited/Teacher Ideas Press. Copyright © 2006.

Powder Your Wigs

(Introduction)
From the Conestoga wagons to the old Kentucky rifles
And the fancy silver snuffboxes they made,
The cooper and the fuller and all those other artisans
Were very, very skillful at their trades.

(Chorus)
So - o - o - o
X - X - X - X - X - X - X - X
Powder your wigs and tip your hats to the craftsmen long ago.
What kinds of jobs did they once do? That's what we'd like to show.

(Verses)
X - X - X - X - X - X - X - X
Slash the sword the cutler made; be careful of the sharpened blade.

A locksmith works with grooves and keys, so tumble like his locks do, please.

Help the wainwright earn a meal; go in circles like his wheel.

Fold your middle like the sheets that the bookbinder completes.

Like the chandler, stir the pot. Make the candles; ouch, it's hot!

Ride to town and back, of course, when the blacksmith shoes your horse.

Make a windmill, do not strain. The miller needs to grind the grain.

Sawyers always work in pairs; saw the logs for all the stairs.

Sift the flour and knead the dough. The baker says, "Come on, let's go."

Fire the cannon, ring the bell! The brazier has some bronze to sell.

Tap your boots on down the street; the cobbler makes some happy feet.

(Final Chorus)
X - X - X - X - X - X - X - X
Powder your wigs and tip your hats to the craftsmen long ago.
What kinds of jobs did they once do? That's what we tried to show.

*(**Spotlight off.** Characters exit stage right.)*

Powder Your Wigs

Mary Wheeler

Blacksmith, Wives: From the Con-e-sto-ga wag-ons to the old Ken-tuck-y ri-fles and the fan-cy sil-ver snuff-box-es they made, the coop-er and the ful-ler and all the oth-er ar-ti-sans were ver-y ver-y skill-ful at their trades. All: So,

Dancers perform the actions sung in each verse.

3. Like the chand - ler stir the pot.
4. Make a wind - mill; do not strain. The

Make the can - dles. Ouch, it's hot!
mil - ler needs to grind the grain.

Ride to town and back, of course,
Saw - yers al - ways work in pairs.

when the black - smith shoes your horse.
Saw the logs for all the stairs.

5. Sift the flour and knead the dough. The ba - ker says, "Come on let's go!" - - - - -

Scene 2

*(**Spotlight on Stage Left**—Abigail Adams; Abigail Adams enters as **Blacksmith Shop** closes. As Abigail Adams speaks, remove blacksmith table, and add desk and window to backdrop for Constitutional Convention.)*

Abigail Adams: My name is Abigail Adams, and I am sending a letter to my husband, John Adams, who is attending the Continental Congress in Philadelphia. The date is March 31, 1776.

"In the new Code of Laws which I suppose it will be necessary for you to make I desire you would Remember the Ladies, and be more generous and favourable to them than your ancestors. Do not put such unlimited powers into the hands of the Husbands. Remember all men would be tyrants if they could. If particular care and attention is not paid to the Ladies, we are determined to forment a Rebellion, and will not hold ourselves bound by any laws in which we have no voice, or Representation."

*(**Spotlight off.** Abigail Adams exits. As Abigail Adams is speaking, James Madison and Gouverneur Morris should secretly take their places in front of their picture. Main characters reenter.)*

*(Choir sings **Constitutional Convention,** chorus only)*

Constitutional Convention

(Chorus)

Constitutional Convention! Constitutional Convention!
To Madison and Washington
And delegates from all those states
We thank you
For going to
The Constitutional Convention.

From *13 Colonies! 13 Years! Integrating Content Standards and the Arts to Teach the American Revolution.* By Mary Wheeler and Jill Terlep. Music by Mary Wheeler. Illustrations by Jill Terlep. Westport, CT: Libraries Unlimited/Teacher Ideas Press. Copyright © 2006.

Act 5: CONSTITUTIONAL CONVENTION

Scene 1

Picture

**[James Madison and Gouverneur Morris
at the Constitutional Convention]**

James Madison and Gouverneur Morris are "frozen."

(Spotlight on center stage; *Poppa, Elvin, Dora Bell, and Tia are staring at "picture" of James Madison and Gouverneur Morris.)*

Poppa: It's our last picture, everyone, and you're looking at members of the Constitutional Convention, James Madison and Gouverneur Morris. It is the summer of 1787.

James Madison: These Articles of Confederation are not working. We can't pay our war debts or get respect from other countries. We need a Constitution and a federal system of government.

Gouverneur Morris: Right. We can't use printed money either. Each state has its own currency, but we have no legal tender for everyone.

Elvin: Love me tender; love me tender ...

Dora: Stop, Elvin, stop. That's legal tender, not love me tender.

Tia: *(Sighing)* Oh, Elvin ...

(Enter George Washington.)

Poppa: Look, it's the president of the Constitutional Convention, George Washington.

Gouverneur Morris: Sir, I believe that the Great Compromise that we have reached among our delegates is a good one. Two houses in Congress, one based on population and the other with two members per state, is fair. I am convinced.

George Washington: These decisions haven't been easy, but here at the Grand Convention we are committed to a national government with many checks and balances.

Dora: All of us appreciate and thank you for your work.

Tia: Because of you, our country is the greatest.

(Sing Constitutional Convention)

Constitutional Convention

Constitutional Convention! Constitutional Convention!
To Madison and Washington
And delegates from all those states
We thank you
For going to
The Constitutional Convention.

Said Madison to Washington, "We want you to preside.
These Articles don't work although our 13 states have tried.
We need a Constitution and our country unified."

"I'll lead this Grand Convention, then," George Washington replied.

Constitutional Convention! Constitutional Convention!
To Madison and Washington
And delegates from all those states
We thank you
For going to
The Constitutional Convention.

Said Madison to Washington, "The Connecticut Compromise
Ensures each state an equal vote, regardless of its size."

"Two houses," answered Washington, "who make our laws is wise.
This governmental framework is the best we can devise."

Constitutional Convention! Constitutional Convention!
To Madison and Washington
And delegates from all those states
We thank you
For going to
The Constitutional Convention.
THANK YOU!

From *13 Colonies! 13 Years! Integrating Content Standards and the Arts to Teach the American Revolution.* By Mary Wheeler and Jill Terlep. Music by Mary Wheeler. Illustrations by Jill Terlep. Westport, CT: Libraries Unlimited/Teacher Ideas Press. Copyright © 2006.

Constitutional Convention

Mary Wheeler

Tia: Sirs, we really mean it. Thank you.

Elvin: *(Imitation)* Thank you. Thank you very, very much.

George Washington: On behalf of 55 delegates who have been working here in Philadelphia on this Constitution during this summer, you're welcome.

(Bell rings offstage)

Elvin: Listen. The bell is ringing again here in Philadelphia.

Dora: Yes, that bell rang at the Declaration signing, the end of the American Revolution, and when the Constitution was written. It has become a symbol of our country and has rung on important occasions throughout history. We call it the Liberty Bell. The words on the bell say, "Proclaim liberty throughout the land and unto all the inhabitants thereof."

Tia: Another famous American symbol is the bald eagle, and in 1782 it was chosen as our national emblem.

Elvin: Benjamin Franklin wanted the turkey to be our national emblem.

James Madison: I'm glad that it's the eagle, Elvin. We hope our people unite behind this Constitution, and we hope our country soars like an eagle.

From *13 Colonies! 13 Years! Integrating Content Standards and the Arts to Teach the American Revolution.* By Mary Wheeler and Jill Terlep. Music by Mary Wheeler. Illustrations by Jill Terlep. Westport, CT: Libraries Unlimited/Teacher Ideas Press. Copyright © 2006.

Sing in a Circle

Come, let's sing in a circle.
See our eagle soar.
Come, let's sing in a circle.
Freedom evermore!

Our country has many colors.
Each person has a view,
But the voice of our America
Is always red, white, and blue.

Come, let's sing in a circle.
See our eagle soar.
Come, let's sing in a circle.
Freedom evermore!

Our people have disagreements,
But we're united throughout the land
That the strength of our America
Is the liberty for which we stand.

Come, let's sing in a circle.
See our eagle soar.
Come, let's sing in a circle.
Freedom evermore!

We say what we believe in.
We fear not another day.
We give thanks for our America
And for livin' in the USA.

Come, let's sing in a circle.
See our eagle soar.
Come, let's sing in a circle.
Freedom evermore!

Sing in a Circle

Mary Wheeler

All: Our coun-try has man-y col-ors. Each per-son has a view but the

voice of our Am-er-i-ca is al-ways red, white, and blue.

Come let's sing in a cir - cle. See our eag-le soar. Come let's sing in a cir - cle. Free-dom ev-er more.

Scene 2

*(**In spotlight, George Washington** walks to **stage left** as **Constitutional Convention** ends. As George Washington speaks, remove desk and window, and add the American flag to backdrop for Finale.)*

George Washington: On April 30, 1789, I was inaugurated as the first president of the United States of America. I took the oath of office at Federal Hall in New York City. From my inaugural address:

"the preservation of the sacred fire of liberty and the destiny of the republican model of government are justly considered, perhaps, as 'deeply', as 'finally', staked on the experiment entrusted to the hands of the American people."

*(**Spotlight off.** George Washington exits. Main characters reenter.)*

From *13 Colonies! 13 Years! Integrating Content Standards and the Arts to Teach the American Revolution.* By Mary Wheeler and Jill Terlep. Music by Mary Wheeler. Illustrations by Jill Terlep. Westport, CT: Libraries Unlimited/Teacher Ideas Press. Copyright © 2006.

Act 6: FINALE

*(**Spotlight on center stage:** Poppa, Elvin, Dora Bell, and Tia are onstage.)*

Poppa: Well, that's the story, everyone. Because of our courageous ancestors—tea, paper, bells, and stamps—and because of all the dedicated American colonists, we have a wonderful, independent, and a free country in which to live.

Elvin: Wow! We have come a long way. What progress! And I even have my own stamp now!

Poppa: *(Dreaming)* And look at all the different kinds of glass we have. I especially like those glamorous perfume bottles . . . Harrummph *(Clears voice, slightly embarrassed)*. Uhh, we even recycle now.

Elvin: And I don't have to work as hard as stamps used to. I'm only used on the U.S. Mail now. Come to think of it, we're doing such a great job at the U.S. Mail, maybe we ought to raise the price of stamps.

Dora: You're joking, right, Elvin? Sometimes it takes a long time for me to get my letter.

Elvin: Don't be cruel.

Poppa: Just keep working on your delivery, Elvin.

Elvin: *(Looking upset)* Well, we are really improving one part of the mail.

Dora: What part is that?

Elvin: Return to sender.

Tia: In those 13 years, important events in the early 13 colonies surely did shape our nation's future.

Dora: 13 colonies, 13 years. Gosh, I always thought 13 was an unlucky number.

Poppa: Not for us! From 1776 to 1789, that was the time that the United States of America was born.

All: Hooray! 13 colonies! 13 years!

(All stage actors reenter the stage and gather around Poppa, Elvin, Dora Bell, and Tia to join in singing 13 Colonies! 13 Years!)

(Sing ***13 Colonies! 13 Years!***)

13 Colonies! 13 Years!

Chimes—(Ring—Ring—Ring—Ring)
1776 to 1789
Chimes—(Ring—Ring—Ring—- Ring)

13 colonies, 13 years! 13 colonies, 13 years!
They started with a declaration,
Ended with inauguration.
Let us have a celebration, NOW!
13 colonies, 13 years! 13 colonies, 13 years!

Massachusetts, Pennsylvania, Connecticut, and Delaware,
North Carolina, South Carolina, Georgia—they all were there.

New Hampshire, New York, and New Jersey –
Everywhere church bells were heard.
Maryland, Virginia, and tiny Rhode Island—
They all opposed King George the Third.

Chimes—(Ring—Ring—Ring—Ring)
1776 to 1789
Chimes—(Ring—Ring—Ring—Ring)

13 colonies, 13 years! 13 colonies, 13 years!
They started with a declaration,
Ended with inauguration.
Let us have a celebration, NOW!
13 colonies, 13 years! 13 colonies, 13 years!
13 Colonies, 13 Years!

(LIGHTS OUT; KETTLE DRUM ROLL)

Announcer: Ladies and Gentlemen. Elvin Stamp has left the building.

(LIGHTS ON IMMEDIATELY—EVERY LIGHT POSSIBLE)

THE END

From *13 Colonies! 13 Years! Integrating Content Standards and the Arts to Teach the American Revolution.* By Mary Wheeler and Jill Terlep. Music by Mary Wheeler. Illustrations by Jill Terlep. Westport, CT: Libraries Unlimited/Teacher Ideas Press. Copyright © 2006.

13 Colonies! 13 Years!

Mary Wheeler

From *13 Colonies! 13 Years! Integrating Content Standards and the Arts to Teach the American Revolution.* By Mary Wheeler and Jill Terlep. Music by Mary Wheeler. Illustrations by Jill Terlep. Westport, CT: Libraries Unlimited/Teacher Ideas Press. Copyright © 2006.

Teacher Management

Audition Information for the Teacher

Before holding auditions, tell the students about the *13 Colonies! 13 Years!* production. Build up enthusiasm ahead of time by describing the characters and telling about the story.

Elvin Stamp: (stamp) *Stamp Act of 1765* required <u>stamps</u> on almost all printed materials.

Poppa Bottle: (pop bottle) *Townshend Duties of 1767* taxed <u>glass</u> and more.

Tia Bagwell: (tea bag) *Tea Act of 1773* taxed <u>tea</u>.

Dora Bell: (door bell) *Liberty Bell* and other <u>bells</u> rang in celebrations.

In the story, the characters search for their roots and discover a lot about our nation's struggle for independence during the years from 1776 to 1789. Along the way, they meet George Washington, Ben Franklin, Phillis Wheatley, Abigail Adams, and others.

Announce the song titles.

13 Colonies! 13 Years!   *Frankly, Mr. Franklin*
The Ballad of John Paul Jones   *Independence Battle Rap*
Wisdom Is Higher   *Powder Your Wigs*
Constitutional Convention   *Sing in a Circle*

Let the students discover that they will learn about the American Revolution in a very unique and exciting way. Tell them that the finished product is going to take a lot of work, but they will create memories for themselves and their friends for a lifetime!

Tips for the director:

• Give the students a choice of how they want to contribute—act, work behind the stage, sing in the choir, etc. Have them decide and note it a few days before the auditions.

• Use the ***Audition Letter to the Students*** to give details on the audition process.
  The audition letter provides the following choices:

  _____ *Be a main character (a lot of memorizing)—Poppa, Dora, Tia, and Elvin*
  _____ *Be a supporting character (less memorizing)—Patrick Henry, Benjamin Franklin, Thomas*
  Jefferson, George Washington, etc.
  _____ *Appear on stage, but say only 1 line or 2 lines—extra soldiers*
  _____ *Be a dancer*
  _____ *Sing in the choir*
  _____ *Work in the stage crew*
  _____ *Anything else you want to say?*

• Consider having two sets of main characters, for Acts 1–3 and for Acts 4–6.

• Enlist adult help in conducting the auditions.

From *13 Colonies! 13 Years! Integrating Content Standards and the Arts to Teach the American Revolution.* By Mary Wheeler and Jill Terlep. Music by Mary Wheeler. Illustrations by Jill Terlep. Westport, CT: Libraries Unlimited/Teacher Ideas Press. Copyright © 2006.

- A couple of days ahead of time, give the first two pages of the play to everyone who wants to try out. Let them know that even though they are reading the part of Dora, for example, that is not necessarily the part for which they will be chosen.

- Conduct the auditions in front of an audience, including other children.

- Rate the students as they try out.

- Make sure the students who get singing parts can carry a tune!

Lights! Camera! Action!

Our class is ready to begin rehearsals for a play about the American Revolution. It is a musical about a stamp, glass, bell, and tea bag that come to life! The characters, Elvin Stamp, Poppa Bottle, Dora Bell, and Tia Bagwell, search for their roots, and as they learn about their ancestors, the actors discover interesting facts about their forefathers. The years when our country struggled for independence, 1776–1789, were so important in our nation's history. We'll all help Dora ring in the celebration for "13 Colonies! 13 Years!"

*Producing this play takes work, but it will be a **lot** of fun. It's time for you to start thinking about how you want to be involved.*

On _____, we will hold auditions and select the stage crew. For the auditions, you will read a passage from the play. Attached sheets include your audition script. If you're trying out for a singing part, you may be asked to sing a short song. Try out your lines or tune in front of a mirror, or better yet, grab a friend or family member and ham it up!

We will be looking for acting qualities like enthusiasm, expression, and timing. So let's get started. You are going to play a special part in this production! Good luck!

Here's a list of songs that we will perform in the play.

13 Colonies! 13 Years!   *Frankly, Mr. Franklin*
The Ballad of John Paul Jones   *Independence Battle Rap*
Wisdom Is Higher   *Powder Your Wigs*
Constitutional Convention   *Sing in a Circle*

- -

Name_____

What would you like to do?

_____ Be a main character (a lot of memorizing)—Poppa, Dora, Tia, and Elvin

_____ Be a supporting character (less memorizing)—Thomas Jefferson, Ben Franklin, etc.

_____ Appear on stage, but only say one or two lines—extra soldiers, etc.

_____ Be a dancer

_____ Sing in the choir

_____ Work with the stage crew—lighting, prop management, directing, etc.

Other ideas or comments: _____

_____

_____

_____

From *13 Colonies! 13 Years! Integrating Content Standards and the Arts to Teach the American Revolution.* By Mary Wheeler and Jill Terlep. Music by Mary Wheeler. Illustrations by Jill Terlep. Westport, CT: Libraries Unlimited/Teacher Ideas Press. Copyright © 2006.

Audition Evaluation Form

Student Name_____

Rate from 1 to 5, with a 5 being great.

Timing	Expression	Enthusiasm	Ability	Voice Control	Overall

Comments:_____

_____

_____

- -

Student Name_____

Rate from 1 to 5, with a 5 being great.

Timing	Expression	Enthusiasm	Ability	Voice Control	Overall

Comments:_____

_____

_____

- -

Student Name_____

Rate from 1 to 5, with a 5 being great.

Timing	Expression	Enthusiasm	Ability	Voice Control	Overall

Comments:_____

_____

_____

From *13 Colonies! 13 Years! Integrating Content Standards and the Arts to Teach the American Revolution.* By Mary Wheeler and Jill Terlep. Music by Mary Wheeler. Illustrations by Jill Terlep. Westport, CT: Libraries Unlimited/Teacher Ideas Press. Copyright © 2006.

Cast

Announcer

Elvin

Dora

Poppa

Tia

Benjamin Franklin

George Washington

Thomas Paine

Patrick Henry

Phillis Wheatley

Abigail Adams

Thomas Jefferson

John Adams

Molly Pitcher

Soldier

Blacksmith

Cobbler's Wife

Miller's Wife

James Madison

Governeur Morris

Dancers

Songs

_____

_____

13 Colonies! 13 Years!:

_____

_____

Frankly, Mr. Franklin:

_____

_____

The Ballad of John Paul Jones:

_____

_____

Independence Battle Rap:

_____

_____

Wisdom Is Higher:

_____

_____

Powder Your Wigs:

_____

_____

Constitutional Convention:

_____

_____

Sing in a Circle:

_____

_____

Dear Parents,

Our group is about to begin work on an educational musical, *13 Colonies! 13 Years!*, that will be presented to the school and community. This program is unique because students and audiences will learn about American Revolutionary history as the musical is being practiced and performed. Each song, each storyline is written to inform the cast and audience about the years 1776–1789. While the project will end with a theatrical performance, it will also expand into the classroom. Historical facts and concepts will be taught as the show is being rehearsed.

The class will have fun and **learn** as they perform the songs. The musical contains lyrics that have been carefully researched, and every word is intended to instruct as well as entertain. The students can look forward to performing the following songs:

- Memorize the names of the 13 colonies along with Elvin Stamp, and do it rock 'n roll style in *13 Colonies! 13 Years!*

- Can Benjamin Franklin offer advice for solving today's problems? Of course. In *Frankly, Mr. Franklin,* the diplomat spouts quotations from his own *Almanack.*

- "I have not yet begun to fight!" In *The Ballad of John Paul Jones* the naval officer shouts those stirring words, and we celebrate his bravery.

- From Lexington to Concord to victory at Yorktown, be a Yankee Doodle and march to the cadence of *Independence Battle Rap.*

- *Wisdom Is Higher*—so climb the steps with Phillis Wheatley, African American poet.

- Get ready for lots of action with *Powder Your Wigs.* Every stage and choir member does aerobic movements that match the motions of colonial craftsmen.

- Thank George Washington, James Madison, Gouverneur Morris, and all the delegates to the *Constitutional Convention.*

- In *Sing in a Circle,* rally around the soaring American eagle.

We believe this will be a tremendous opportunity for your child to learn American Revolutionary history and display his or her talents, and we hope you are as excited as we are with the educational musical. We'll try to keep you informed as we proceed, and we look forward to seeing you at our formal presentation.

Sincerely,

From *13 Colonies! 13 Years! Integrating Content Standards and the Arts to Teach the American Revolution.* By Mary Wheeler and Jill Terlep. Music by Mary Wheeler. Illustrations by Jill Terlep. Westport, CT: Libraries Unlimited/Teacher Ideas Press. Copyright © 2006.

Dear Parents,

Earlier, you received a letter from our group telling you that we were beginning to work on an educational musical, *13 Colonies! 13 Years!* This experience is a tremendous opportunity for your child to learn about the American Revolution and display his or her talents. Producing a program of this magnitude is a big project, but it is also a fun one. Not only will your child learn a lot about this important period in our nation's history, but he or she will be creating memories to last a lifetime!

A lot of time and effort go into the production of such a show, and we will do our best to accomplish as much as we can. As we are proceeding with practices and during the performances, we may be calling on volunteers to help us attain our goals. If you would like to help and can provide some time, we would appreciate your completing this survey and returning the paper with your child.

Please indicate with a checkmark any way you can and would like to volunteer.

_____ Making costumes

_____ Decorating scenery

_____ Helping groups or individuals practice performances

_____ Managing sound systems

_____ Showing spotlights

_____ Copying papers for scripts, worksheets, letters, etc.

_____ Monitoring written work

_____ Organizing papers, props, children, etc. for the performance

_____ Designing and making programs

_____ Planning an "It's a Wrap" Party

_____ Providing snacks for practices or the final party

_____ Cleaning up

_____ Directing or accompanying music practices

Please note any other skills, talents, or services that you could offer.

_____

_____

_____

Telephone_____

Email _____

Volunteer's
Name_____

We appreciate your help! We will contact you if we can use your services. Thank you.

Dear Staff,

On _____ our group will present a dress rehearsal of the musical program, *13 Colonies! 13 Years!*, to the school. You are cordially invited to bring your class. The presentation will start at _____.

In addition to presenting a musical, our group has been learning in the classroom about the American Revolution, and we would like to share some of the history with your students. To help other classes learn more, here is some information about the production.

Synopsis

A stamp, glass, bell, and tea bag come to life! Curious about their ancestors, Elvin Stamp, Poppa Bottle, Dora Bell, and Tia Bagwell search for their roots, and in the process they learn about the American Revolution. Through old pictures belonging to Poppa, the memorable characters discover interesting facts about their forefathers and our country's early struggle for independence. Those years, 1776–1789, were important in our nation's history, and everyone helps Dora ring in the celebration for *13 Colonies! 13 Years!*

The dialogue, action, and songs come together to teach the audience about the American Revolution, as we entertain them. This is what your students will learn:

Act 1

Scene 1: INTRODUCTION
The Stamp Act of 1765 made the colonists angry when it taxed such items as tea and glass, and the main characters decide to look back on the Revolutionary years of 1776–1789. Learn the names of the 13 original colonies as the group sings *13 Colonies! 13 Years!*

Scene 2: Thomas Paine
Thomas Paine calls for independence from Britain when he quotes from his pamphlet, *Common Sense*.

Act 2

Scene 1: DECLARATION OF INDEPENDENCE
Standing beside the Liberty Bell, Thomas Jefferson, John Adams, and Benjamin Franklin discuss the Declaration of Independence. Benjamin Franklin offers advice from his *Almanack* in *Frankly, Mr. Franklin*.

Scene 2: Patrick Henry
Patrick Henry speaks to the Virginia House of Burgesses in the spring of 1775 and says, "but as for me, give me liberty, or give me death."

Act 3

Scene 1: BATTLE OF MONMOUTH
It's the Battle of Monmouth, and our characters sing their praises in *The Ballad of John Paul Jones*, a famous naval hero. Next, Molly Pitcher and a soldier tell us all about the Revolutionary Battles in *Independence Battle Rap*.

Scene 2: Phillis Wheatley
An African American slave who became a famous poet, Phillis Wheatley, sings *Wisdom Is Higher*.

From *13 Colonies! 13 Years! Integrating Content Standards and the Arts to Teach the American Revolution.* By Mary Wheeler and Jill Terlep. Music by Mary Wheeler. Illustrations by Jill Terlep. Westport, CT: Libraries Unlimited/Teacher Ideas Press. Copyright © 2006.

Act 4

Scene 1: BLACKSMITH SHOP

Get ready for lots of action with *Powder Your Wigs*. Every stage and choir member does aerobic movements that match the motions of colonial craftsmen, such as a cutler, bookbinder, miller, sawyer, brazier, etc.

Scene 2: Abigail Adams

Abigail Adams sends a letter to her husband, John, reminding him to "Remember the Ladies."

Act 5

Scene 1: CONSTITUTIONAL CONVENTION

Thank George Washington, James Madison, Gouverneur Morris, and all of the delegates to the *Constitutional Convention*.

Scene 2: George Washington

It's Federal Hall, New York City, April 30, 1789, and we witness the inauguration speech of our first president, George Washington.

Act 6

Finale: Rally around the soaring American eagle in *Sing in a Circle* with all the cast and choir members.

The program will probably last about an hour, and we will do our best to educate and entertain!

Sincerely,

Prop Checklist

☐ Dora's door

☐ Black shoes

☐ Horseshoe

☐ Rubber mallet

☐ Handbell

☐ Doorbell

☐ Wooden stick (rammer)

☐ Speeches to be read (Patrick Henry, George Washington, Phillis Wheatley, Declaration of Independence, Abigail Adams, Thomas Paine)

☐ Drum or keyboard for cadence

☐ Tape recorder/CD sound effects

☐ American flag

☐ _____

☐ _____

☐ _____

☐ _____

☐ _____

☐ _____

☐ _____

☐ _____

☐ _____

Performance Checklist

☐ Door and picture onstage

☐ Ticket takers with tickets and money box

☐ Sound coordinator

☐ Lighting person

☐ Videographer

☐ Tables and chairs for ticket takers, sound coordinator, spotlight person

☐ Props prepared and backstage

☐ Program passers with programs

☐ Music/intercom, arriving and leaving

☐ Piano or keyboard in place with music

☐ Microphones and extensions setup

☐ Timeline displayed

☐ Backdrops and related items in place

☐ Choir chairs

☐ Audience seating

☐ Spotlight

☐ Light for piano

☐ Scripts for director, musician, production helpers, etc.

☐ costumes

☐ _____

☐ _____

☐ _____

☐ _____

☐ _____

☐ _____

☐ _____

Bibliography

Axelrod, Dr. Alan, and Charles Phillips. *What Every American Should Know about American History,* 2d ed. Avon, MA: Adams Media, 2004.

Berkin, Carol. *Revolutionary Mothers: Women in the Struggle for America's Independence.* New York: Alfred A. Knopf, 2005.

Bloom, Sol. *The Story of the Constitution.* Washington, DC: National Archives and Records Administration, 1986.

Boller, Paul F., Jr. *Presidential Anecdotes,* rev. ed. New York: Oxford University Press, 1996.

Bowen, Catherine Drinker. *Miracle at Philadelphia.* Boston: Little, Brown, and Company, 1986.

Brownell, David. *Heroes of the American Revolution.* Santa Barbara, CA: Bellerophon Books, 1991.

Davis, Kenneth C. *Don't Know Much about History.* New York: HarperCollins, 2003.

Dray, Philip. *Stealing God's Thunder: Benjamin Franklin's Lightning Rod and the Invention of America.* New York: Random House, 2005.

Earle, Alice Morse. *Child Life in Colonial Days.* Stockbridge, MA: Berkshire House Publishers, 1993.

Edgar, Walter B. *Partisans and Redcoats: The Southern Conflict That Turned the Tide of the American Revolution.* New York: William Morrow, 2001.

Ferris, Robert G., and James H. Charleton. *The Signers of the Constitution.* Flagstaff, AZ: Interpretive Publications, 2001.

Frank, Sid, and Arden Davis Melick. *The Presidents: Tidbits & Trivia, Revised Edition Including President Ronald Reagan.* Maplewood, NJ: Hammond, 1990.

Franklin, Benjamin. *The Autobiography of Benjamin Franklin and Other Writings.* Edited and with Introduction by Kenneth Silverman. New York: Penguin Books, 1986.

Franklin, Benjamin. *Poor Richard's Almanack.* Mount Vernon, NY: Peter Pauper Press.

Fredericks, Anthony. *Readers Theatre for American History.* Englewood, CO: Teacher Ideas Press, 2001.

Fritz, Jean. *Shhh! We're Writing the Constitution.* New York: G.P. Putnam's Sons, 1987.

Fritz, Jean. *What's the Big Idea, Ben Franklin?* New York: Coward-McCann, 1976.

Garrison, Webb. *Great Stories of the American Revolution.* Nashville, TN: Rutledge Hill Press, 1990.

Goldstein, Richard. *Mine Eyes Have Seen.* New York: Simon & Schuster, 1997.

Hallahan, William H. *The Day the American Revolution Began: 19 April 1775.* New York: William Morrow, 2000.

Hallahan, William H. *The Day the American Revolution Ended: 19 October 1781.* Hoboken, NJ: John Wiley & Sons, 2004.

Levy, Elizabeth. *...if you were there when They Signed the Constitution.* New York: Scholastic Books, 1992.

Madison, James, Edward Larson, and Michael Winship. *The Constitutional Convention: A Narrative History from the Notes of James Madison.* New York: Modern Library, 2005.

Maestro, Betsy, and Giulio Maestro. *A More Perfect Union: The Story of Our Constitution.* New York: Mulberry Books, 1987.

People in Time and Place. Morristown, NJ/ Needham, MA: Silver Burdett & Ginn, 1991.

Perl, Lila. *It Happened in America.* New York: Henry Holt, 1994.

The Presidents and Their Wives from George Washington to William Jefferson Clinton. Rockville, MD: C.M. Uberman Enterprises, 1997.

The Revolutionary War, A Sourcebook on Colonial America. Edited by Carter Smith. Brookfield, CT: Millbrook Press, 1991.

Richards, Leonard L. *Shay's Rebellion: The American Revolution's Final Battle.* Philadelphia: University of Pennsylvania Press, 2002.

Richards, Norman. *The Story of Bonhomme Richard.* Chicago: Children's Press, 1969.

Stein, R. Conrad. *The Story of Valley Forge.* Chicago: Children's Press, 1985.

The Spirit of Seventy-Six / The Sourcebook of the American Revolution as Told by the Participants. Edited by Henry Steele Commager and Richard B. Morris. New York: Da Capo Press, 1995.

Tunis, Edwin. *Colonial Craftsmen, And the Beginnings of American Industry.* Baltimore, MD: The John Hopkins University Press, 1999.

Urdang, Laurence, editor. *The Timetables of American History.* New York: Simon & Schuster, 1996.

Wall, Charles Cecil. *George Washington, Citizen—Soldier.* Mount Vernon, VA: Mount Vernon Ladies Association, 1988.

Wheatley, Phillis. *Poems of Phillis Wheatley/A Native American and a Slave.* Bedford, MA: Applewood Books, 1969.

Wilson, Jr. Vincent. *The Book of Distinguished American Women.* Brookville, MD*:* American History Research Associates, 1992.

Supplemental Reading

Resources for Students

Allen, Thomas B. *George Washington, Spymaster: How the Americans Outspied the British and Won the Revolutionary War*. Washington, DC: National Geographic Society, 2004.

Ammon, Richard. *Valley Forge*. New York: Holiday House, 2004.

Aronson, Marc. *The Real Revolution: The Global Story of American Independence*. New York: Clarion, 2005.

Barretta, Gene. *Now & Ben: The Modern Inventions of Benjamin Franklin*. New York: Henry Holt, 2006.

Bernstein, Vivian. *America's History: Land of Liberty*. Updated 2001 ed. New York: Oxford University Press, 2001.

Blackwood, Gary. *The Year of the Hangman*. Dutton. New York: Dutton Children's Books, 2002.

Bobrick, Benson. *Fight for Freedom: The American Revolutionary War*. New York: Atheneum Books for Young Readers, 2004.

Brenner, Barbara. *If You Lived in Williamsburg in Colonial Days*. New York: Scholastic, 2000.

Caltrow, David. *We the Kids: The Preamble to the Constitution of the United States*. New York: Dial Books for Young Readers, 2002.

Chandra, Deborah, and Madeleine Comora. *George Washington's Teeth*. New York: Farrar, Straus & Giroux, 2003.

Cheney, Lynne V. *A Time for Freedom: What Happened When in America*. New York: Simon & Schuster, 2005.

Declaration of Independence: The Words That Made America. Illustrated by Sam Fink. New York: Scholastic Reference, 2002.

Egger-Bovet, Howard, and Marlene Smith-Baranzini. *US Kids History: Book of the American Revolution*. Boston: Little, Brown and Company, 1994.

Fleming, Candace. *Ben Franklin's Almanac: Being a True Account of the Good Gentleman's Life*. New York: Atheneum Books for Young Children, 2003.

Fradin, Dennis Brindell. *The Framers: The 39 Stories Behind the U.S. Constitution*. New York: Atheneum Books for Young Children, 2005.

Fradin, Dennis Brindell. *The Signers: The 56 Stories Behind the Declaration of Independence*. New York: Walker, 2002.

Freedman, Russell. *Give Me Liberty!: The Story of the Declaration of Independence.* New York: Holiday House, 2000.

Freedman, Russell. *In Defense of Liberty: The Story of America's Bill of Rights.* New York: Holiday House, 2003.

Furbee, Mary Rodd. *Outrageous Women of Colonial America.* New York: Wiley, 2001.

Giddens, Sandra and Owen. *A Timeline of the Constitutional Convention.* New York: Rosen Central, 2004.

Hakim, Joy. *A History of Us: Book Three: From Colonies to Country, 1735–1791.* 3rd ed. New York: Oxford University Press, 2003.

Harness, Cheryl. *The Remarkable Benjamin Franklin.* Washington, DC: National Geographic Society, 2005.

Harness, Cheryl. *The Revolutionary John Adams.* Washington, DC: National Geographic Society, 2003.

January, Brendan. *Colonial Life.* New York: Children's Press, 2000.

Jurmain, Suzanne Tripp. *George Did It.* New York: Dutton Children's Books, 2005.

Kalman, Bobbie. *Colonial Crafts.* New York: Crabtree Publishing, 1992.

Kalman, Bobbie. *Colonial Life.* New York: Crabtree Publishing, 1992.

Kalman, Bobbie, and John Crossingham. *Colonial Home.* New York: Crabtree Publishing, 2001.

Lasky, Kathryn. *A Voice of Her Own: The Story of Phillis Wheatley, Slave Poet.* Cambridge, MA: Candlewick Press, 2003.

Longfellow, Henry Wadsworth. *The Midnight Ride of Paul Revere.* Brooklyn, NY: Handprint Books, 2001.

Maestro, Betsy, and Giulio Maestro. *Liberty or Death: The American Revolution: 1763–1783.* New York: HarperCollins, 2005.

Marrin, Albert. *George Washington and the Founding of a Nation.* New York: Dutton Children's Books, 2001.

McDonald, Megan. *Saving the Liberty Bell.* New York: Atheneum Books for Young Readers, 2005.

Miller, Brandon Marie. *Declaring Independence: Life During the American Revolution.* Minneapolis: Lerner, 2005

Murray, Stuart. *American Revolution.* Revised ed. New York: DK Children in association with the Smithsonian Institution, 2005.

Pobst, Sandy, with Kevin D. Roberts. *Voices from Colonial America: Virginia, 1607–1776.* Washington, DC: National Geographic Society, 2005.

Schanzer, Rosalyn. *George vs. George: The Revolutionary War as Seen by Both Sides.* Washington, DC: National Geographic Society, 2004.

Sheinkin, Steve. *The American Revolution.* Stamford, CT: Summer Street Press, 2005.

Smith, Lane. *John, Paul, George & Ben.* New York: Hyperion Books for Children, 2006.

Sobel, Syl. *The U.S. Constitution and You.* Hauppauge, NY: Barron's Educational Series, 2001.

Spier, Peter. *We the People, The Constitution of the United States of America.* Garden City, NY: Doubleday, 1987.

St George, Judith. *John and Abigail Adams: An American Love Story.* New York: Holiday House, 2001.

St. George, Judith. *The Journey of the One and Only Declaration of Independence.* New York: Philomel Books, 2005.

Thomson, Sarah L. *Stars and Stripes: The Story of the American Flag.* New York: HarperCollins Publishers, 2003.

Wallner, Alexandra. *Abigail Adams.* New York: Holiday House, 2001.